Good Cooking

Frying Like a Pro

By
Katharina H. Rodriguez

OLIVE AND CLAM COCKTAIL

Use olive meats for this. Olive meats are pieces of olives cut from large olives and packed in jars. There are no stones nor waste. Place in a small bowl

Three tablespoons of chili sauce,
One tablespoon of horseradish,
One tablespoon of lemon juice,
One-quarter cup of olive meats,
One teaspoon of salt,
One teaspoon of paprika,
One tablespoon of grated onion.

Mix thoroughly and then divide into four cocktail glasses. Add three cherrystone or little-neck clams to each glass.

SAUCES

A formula is necessary if the housewife is to have her sauces uniform, so that

One level tablespoon of flour and one cup of milk make a thin sauce, as for soups.

Two level tablespoons of flour and one cup of milk make a thin sauce.

Three level tablespoons of flour and one cup of milk make a medium sauce.

Four tablespoons of flour and one cup of milk make a thick sauce.

Five level tablespoons of flour and one cup of milk make a sauce for cutlets, croquettes, etc.

Use a saucepan that is scoured bright, add the flour to the cold milk and then stir to dissolve, using fork or wire whip to facilitate the process. Never use a spoon for this purpose, as it is impossible to thoroughly dissolve the lumps. Place on the fire and bring to a boil, stirring constantly. Cook for five minutes after the boiling point is reached and then remove from the fire and add seasoning. It is then ready to use. If you desire a butter flavor, add one tablespoonful of butter with the seasoning and stir until melted.

Part milk and water, stock, chicken broth, oyster or clam juice may be used in place of all milk with very good results. When making soups or sauces for meat and vegetable dishes the liquid from the canned vegetables, or the water in which the fresh vegetables were cooked, may be combined with an equal portion of milk.

Many splendid varieties of sauce can be made from the plain cream sauce. For parsley sauce add four tablespoonfuls of finely chopped parsley to one cup of cream sauce.

ONION SAUCE

One-half cupful of cooked onions, rubbed through a coarse sieve, and then add to one cupful of cream sauce.

PIMENTO CREAM SAUCE

Three canned pimentos, rubbed through a fine sieve and then add to one cupful of cream sauce.

SUPREME SAUCE

One cupful of thick cream sauce,
One-half cupful of mushrooms, pared and cut in pieces and parboiled,
Yolk of one egg.

Seasoning well to taste.

CELERY SAUCE

One cup of thick cream sauce,
One cup of finely diced celery, parboiled until tender,
One teaspoon of salt,
One-half teaspoon of paprika.

Blend well.

ADMIRAL SAUCE

One cup of thick cream sauce,
Grated rind of one-quarter lemon,
Two tablespoons of capers,
Two tablespoons of finely chopped parsley,
Juice of one-half lemon,
Two tablespoons of butter.

Stir until well blended and then heat until just below the boiling point. Season.

BEARNAISE SAUCE

One-half cup of thick cream sauce,
Yolks of two eggs,
One teaspoon of grated onion,
Three tablespoons of butter.

Blend well, and now add

One teaspoon of salt,
One-half teaspoon of white pepper,
One-half teaspoon of paprika,
Juice of one lemon.

Stir constantly until scalding hot. This sauce will not curdle if left standing for a few minutes.

CREAM HORSERADISH SAUCE

One cup of medium cream sauce,
Two tablespoons of grated horseradish,
Two tablespoons of lemon juice,
Three tablespoons of finely minced parsley,
One-half teaspoon of mustard,
One-half teaspoon of white pepper,
One teaspoon of salt.

Beat thoroughly to mix.

MAINTENON SAUCE (for au gratin dishes)

One cup of medium cream sauce,
Two tablespoons of grated cheese,
Two tablespoons of finely minced parsley,
One tablespoon of grated onion,
One and one-half teaspoons of salt,
One teaspoonful of paprika,
One-quarter teaspoon of mustard,
One teaspoon of lemon juice.

Blend well.

CHEESE SAUCE

One cup of medium cream sauce.
Four tablespoons of grated cheese,
One teaspoon of salt,
One-half teaspoon of paprika,
One-quarter teaspoon of mustard.

Blend well until the cheese is melted.

MUSTARD SAUCE

One-half cup of medium cream sauce,

Two tablespoons of white wine vinegar,
Yolk of one egg,
One teaspoon of mustard,
One teaspoon of salt,
One-half teaspoon of paprika.

Beat thoroughly to mix and then heat to the boiling point.

In no other part of cookery does the skill of the cook show to advantage as in the way in which the various sauces are prepared and served. To make a perfect sauce is an art in cooking. Many plain foods, as well as the use of leftovers, may, by the addition of a good sauce, be turned into palatable and attractive dishes.

Three or four cupfuls of cream sauce may be made at one time and then poured into a bowl and covered with a damp napkin, and placed in the icebox until needed. The sauce will keep in a cool place for three or four days and will relieve the necessity of making a sauce every day.

To use, measure three-quarters of a cupful of sauce and add one-quarter cupful of hot water. Place in a double boiler to heat, stirring frequently to blend. It is then ready to use. Always use a double boiler in the preparation of sauces made from this cream sauce. This will prevent scorching.

CUCUMBERSAUCE

One cup of thick cream sauce,
One small cucumber, pared and grated,
One and one-half teaspoons of salt,
One teaspoon of paprika.

Heat to the boiling point and then cook for five minutes.

OYSTERSAUCE

One cup of thick cream sauce,
Eight medium-sized oysters, chopped fine,
One teaspoon of finely minced parsley,

One teaspoon of salt,
One teaspoonful of white pepper.

Blend well and then heat to the boiling point, and cook for five minutes.

MUSHROOM SAUCE

Place one and one-half cups of milk in a saucepan and add four tablespoons of flour. Stir until dissolved and then bring to a boil. Cook for five minutes and then add

One cup of diced and parboiled mushrooms,
One well-beaten egg,
One teaspoon of salt,
One teaspoon of paprika,
Three tablespoons of finely chopped parsley.

Beat to mix and then cook for two minutes and use.

PARSLEY SAUCE

One and one-half cups of cream sauce,
One-half cup of finely chopped parsley,
Three tablespoons of butter,
Two teaspoons of salt,
One teaspoon of white pepper.

Beat to mix.

CREOLE SAUCE

One cup of stewed tomatoes,
Three onions,
One green pepper, chopped fine.

Place in a saucepan and cook slowly until the onion and pepper are soft. Rub through a fine sieve and then add

Two tablespoons of cornstarch dissolved in
One-half cup of water,
One teaspoon of salt,
One teaspoon of paprika,
One-fourth teaspoon of mustard.

Bring to a boil and cook slowly for ten minutes and then serve.

TARTARE SAUCE

One-half cup of mayonnaise dressing,
One onion grated,
Five tablespoons of finely chopped parsley,
One sour pickle, chopped fine,
One teaspoon of salt,
One-half teaspoon of mustard,
One-half teaspoon of paprika.

Mix thoroughly and then serve very cold.

HERB SAUCE

Make one and one-half cups of cream sauce and then add

One cup of finely chopped parsley,
One tablespoon of grated onion,
One-half green pepper, minced fine,
One and one-half teaspoons of salt,
One-half teaspoon of pepper.

Simmer slowly for ten minutes.

MINT SAUCE

Shred a bunch of mint fine, and then place in a saucepan and add

Three-quarters cup of water,
One-quarter cup of sugar.

Bring to a boil and cook slowly for ten minutes. Add one-half cupful of white wine vinegar and remove from the fire. Let stand for one-half hour and then strain. Leftover portions may be bottled and the bottles stored in a cool place for future use.

ENGLISH MUSTARD SAUCE

Place in a soup plate

One teaspoon of mustard,
One teaspoon of sugar,
One-half teaspoon of salt,
One-half teaspoon of paprika,
Two tablespoons of salad oil.

Work to a smooth paste, and then slowly beat in three tablespoons of cream and one teaspoon of lemon juice. Beat until thick and then serve.

HOLLANDAISE SAUCE

Four tablespoons of salad oil,
Two tablespoons of vinegar,

One tablespoon of water,
One teaspoon of salt,
One-half teaspoon of paprika.

Heat in a double boiler to the scalding point and then drop in the yolk of an egg. Stir until thick. Use at once. If it should curdle, add one tablespoonful of boiling water and stir constantly until thick.

RAVIGOTTE SAUCE

Chop very fine sufficient parsley. To measure

One-half cup,
One large green pepper,
One onion,
One leek.

Place in a bowl and add

One cup of mayonnaise,
One teaspoon of salt,
One teaspoon of paprika,
One-half teaspoon of mustard,
Two teaspoons of lemon juice.

Blend well to thoroughly mix.

BROILED CHICKEN, BACON GARNISH

Select a plump broiler and then singe. Then split down the back and draw. Wash well. Remove the breast bone. Place in a frying pan, the split side down, and add one cup of water. Cover closely and then steam for ten minutes. Now rub well with shortening. Dust very lightly with flour. Broil for twenty minutes, turning every four minutes; lift to a hot platter, brush with melted butter and garnish with bacon.

EMINCE OF GIBLETS

Cook the giblets and neck, then cool. Mince fine and add two hard-boiled eggs and one and one-half cups of cream sauce, and

Two tablespoons finely minced parsley,
One and one-half teaspoons of salt,
One teaspoon of paprika.

Heat to boiling point and then simmer slowly for ten minutes.

CHICKEN POT ROAST, CEDAR HOLLOW STYLE

Select a fat stewing chicken and then singe and draw. Wash and wipe with a clean cloth. Place in a fireless cooker or cook until tender. Now rub with shortening and dust with flour and brown in hot fat in a deep saucepan. Turn the chicken frequently so that it can be browned on all sides. When the chicken is nicely browned, add

Four tablespoons of flour,
Three cups of chicken stock,
One-half cup of grated carrot,
Two green peppers chopped fine,
One-half cup of finely minced onions.

Simmer slowly for one-half hour. Season and serve.

CHICKEN AND RICE CURRY

Wash one-half cupful of rice in plenty of warm water and then drain. Rinse again and then place in a saucepan and add two and one-half cups of boiling water. Cook gently until the grains are soft and the water absorbed. Now place

One teaspoon of bacon or chicken fat,
Three tablespoons of flour

in an iron frying pan and brown carefully until a dark brown, then add

One and one-half cups of chicken stock,

Two large onions, chopped very fine,
Two tablespoons of catsup,
One tablespoon of Worcestershire sauce,
Three-quarters teaspoon of curry powder,
One teaspoon of salt.

Cook gently to the boiling point and then add one cupful of shredded chicken meat and the prepared rice. Heat slowly until very hot and then turn on a hot platter and garnish with finely shredded parsley, then serve.

HOW TO PREPARE CHICKEN FOR CHICKEN SALAD OR COLD CUTS

Singe and draw the chicken and then cut as for fricasseeing. Now place the back of the carcass, giblets and the thighs and legs in a saucepan and cover with cold water. Bring to a boil and then turn into a colander and place under cold running water. Then drop into a saucepan containing boiling water and cook for ten minutes. Blanch in the colander under cold running water. Repeat this three times and then add the balance of the chicken and cook slowly until tender. Cool in the liquid. Pick the meat from the neck and back of the carcass and mince the giblets fine. Put the skin through the food chopper. Use this for chicken loaf.

CHICKEN LOAF

Use two cups of mince prepared from the skin, giblets and meat from the carcass.

One and one-half cups of cold cooked oatmeal,
One onion, grated,
One-half teaspoon of powdered thyme,
One-half teaspoon mustard,
Three teaspoons of salt,
One and one-half teaspoons of paprika,
Two green peppers chopped fine,
Four tablespoons of chicken fat,
One egg,
One-half cup of chicken stock.

Mix thoroughly and then pour into a well-greased and floured loaf-shaped pan. Set this pan in a larger one containing hot water. Bake in a moderate oven for one and one-quarter hours. Serve hot with a cream, tomato or brown sauce, or serve cold with a garnish of asparagus and with Hollandaise, mayonnaise or cream horseradish sauce.

ROAST CHICKEN

Prepare the chicken. Fill with

Two stalks of celery,
Two onions,
One cupful of bread crumbs,
One fagot of potherbs,
Two tablespoons of butter, or shortening,
One egg.

Put the celery, onions and potherbs through the food chopper. Mix bread crumbs, butter and beaten egg. Fill into the chicken and then sew the opening. Shape and roast in a moderate oven for twenty minutes to the pound. Baste every ten minutes the first half hour, then every twenty minutes until the chicken is cooked.

ENCHILDAS

Place

One cup of flour,
One-quarter cup of cornflour,
One teaspoon of salt,
One tablespoon of shortening,

in a mixing bowl. Sift to mix and then add sufficient water to make a dough. Break the dough into pieces the size of a large walnut, and then roll out very thin. You may bake the tortillas on the iron griddle on the top of the stove or fry them in a pan, using a little shortening. Keep on a clean towel until all are fried. Now place two ounces of grated cheese in a bowl and add two onions that have been cooked until tender in two tablespoons of shortening and

One-half cup of finely chopped cold meat, preferably chicken,
Two tablespoons of chili sauce.

Mix to blend and then spread the tortillas with this mixture. Roll or fold and then pour over them more hot chili sauce.

CHICKEN GUMBO OKRA

Clean and cut the chicken for stewing. Brown quickly in hot fat. Lift to a deep saucepan and add

Two quarts of water,
Four onions,
One bay leaf,
Two cloves.

Cook until the chicken is tender. Now thicken the liquid slightly with cornstarch. Season with

Red pepper and salt,
Two tablespoons of fine chopped parsley,
One-half teaspoon of thyme,
One tablespoon of gumbo or file,
Two cups of cooked okra.

Send to the table at once and serve with plenty of boiled rice.

Note.—Gumbo, or file, is a powder made and sold in Louisiana. It is composed of young sassafras leaves. File can be purchased in fancy grocery stores.

CHICKEN MOUSSE

Put sufficient boiled cold chicken through a food chopper to measure two cups, using the fine knife. Place in a bowl and add

Two teaspoons of grated onion,
One-half teaspoon of paprika,
One teaspoon salt.

Mix well and then soak one and one-half level tablespoons of gelatine in four tablespoons of cold water for twenty minutes, then add one-half cup of boiling chicken stock. Simmer slowly for five minutes and then strain into the prepared chicken meat. Stir until it is cool, and then fold in one cup of whipped cream. Pour into small custard cups that have been rinsed with cold water. Set in a cold place for six hours to mould. Unmould in a nest of crisp lettuce leaves.

POULTRY

To roast young chickens and guineas: singe, draw and prepare the fowl; now rub the entire bird well with plenty of shortening. Dust very lightly with flour, place in pan in hot oven for fifteen minutes; now turn the fowl breast down in the pan and reduce the heat of the oven to moderate. Baste every ten minutes with following mixture:

One pint boiling water,
Two tablespoons butter.

When fowl is tender turn on back to allow breast to brown, basting every five minutes. Placing the breast of the chicken down in the pan throws the bony structure of the carcass to the intense heat of the oven. The constant basting causes the moisture to permeate the dry white meat, making it juicy and tender.

If you desire, lay a few strips of bacon over the breast when browning it, just before you remove it from oven. It will improve the flavor.

CHICKEN SALAD SANDWICHES

Cut the meat from a three-and-one-half-pound cold boiled fowl and then put through the food chopper, using the coarsest knife. Place in a bowl, adding one medium-sized head of lettuce, shredded fine. Place

One small onion, grated,
One green pepper, minced fine,
One and one-half cups of mayonnaise or salad dressing,
Two and one-half teaspoons of salt,
One teaspoon of paprika.

Mix and then fill into quart fruit jars. This amount will make from forty to fifty sandwiches.

BAKED SQUAB

Split the squab down the back with a sharp knife and then clean thoroughly. Wash well and wipe dry. Place in cool place until needed.

Mince the giblets fine and then parboil. Now soak stale bread until soft. Squeeze dry and measure three-quarters of a cupful. Place in frying pan and add

One-quarter cup of finely minced celery leaves,
Minced giblets,
One onion, minced fine,
One teaspoon of salt,
One teaspoon of poultry seasoning,
Four tablespoons of shortening.

Cook gently until onions are soft and then cool. Fill into squab and then sew up with darning needle and stout string. Rub with shortening and dust with cornflour. Place in a hot oven and bake, basting with boiling water.

When the back is well browned reduce the heat and turn the bird on its back and let brown slowly, allowing fifty-five minutes for cooking the squab. Filling may be placed in chicken or guinea if desired.

TENNESSEE TURKEY HASH

Cut sufficient turkey in one-half inch blocks to measure two cupfuls. Now add

One cup of diced celery,
One onion, minced fine,
One tablespoon of butter,
One tablespoon of cornstarch.

Mix thoroughly, then add

One-half cup of boiling water.

Cook slowly until the meat is very tender, then serve garnished with finely chopped parsley and hot cornmeal waffles.

FILLET OF CHICKEN, POINDEXTER

Singe, draw and then wash thoroughly a large stewing chicken and then cook until tender. Let cool. Now cut the wings and take out the bones, breaking as little as possible. Cut the breast into slices a little larger than an oyster and remove the legs and thighs. Remove the bones and then cut the meat into neat filets. If the meat breaks apart, press firmly together and then season, roll in flour and dip in beaten egg; then roll in fine bread crumbs. Press firmly. Fry until golden brown in hot fat. This may be prepared early in the day and then set in the oven to heat.

CHICKEN TAMALES

Soak the corn husks in cold water for two hours. Place in a saucepan

Two cups of chicken stock,
One teaspoon of salt,
Three-quarters cup of cornmeal.

Cook until thick mush, cool and then place in a bowl

Three-quarters cup of finely chopped chicken meat,
One onion, chopped fine,
Two green peppers, chopped fine,
Six olives, chopped fine,
Two dozen seeded raisins.

Mix thoroughly and then drain the corn husks. Spread a layer of the corn mush on one part, place a tablespoon of the chicken filling in place and then cover with more corn mush, forming a roll a little larger than a sausage. Tie securely in corn husk and place in a steamer or a double boiler and cook for one and one-quarter hours. Other meat may be used to replace the chicken and water may be used in place of the chicken stock to make the mush.

HONEY RECIPES

CANDIED SWEET POTATOES WITH HONEY

Place in an iron frying pan

Three-quarters cup of honey,
Two tablespoons of shortening,
One-quarter teaspoon of mace,
One-quarter teaspoon of cinnamon.

Bring to a boil and cook until it becomes thick, then add six boiled sweet potatoes. Turn them frequently in syrup, adding four tablespoons of water to prevent burning. Cook slowly for twenty minutes.

NOTE.—Have the potatoes boiled and then peeled, and ready waiting before putting the honey in the pan.

HONEY RICE PUDDING

Wash one-half cup of rice thoroughly and then cook until tender and the water absorbed in two and one-half cups of water. Turn into a baking dish and add

One cup of honey,
Three cups of milk,
One well-beaten egg,
One-half teaspoon of nutmeg.

Stir to thoroughly mix and then bake in a slow oven for thirty minutes.

HONEY ICING

Boil one cup of honey until it forms a soft ball when tried in cold water. Then pour in a fine stream upon the stiffly beaten white of one egg. Beat until the mixture thickens and then spread on the cake.

NUT HONEY CAKE

Place in a mixing bowl

One cup of honey,
One cup of brown sugar,
Yolks of two eggs,
Nine tablespoons of shortening.

Cream together and then add

Three-quarters cup of sour milk,
One and one-half teaspoons of baking soda.

Dissolve the baking soda in the sour milk, then add

Four cups of flour,
Two teaspoons of cinnamon,
One-half teaspoon of allspice,
One-half teaspoon of cloves,
One-half teaspoon of nutmeg,
One cup of finely chopped raisins,
One cup of finely chopped nuts,
One tablespoon of baking powder.

Mix thoroughly and then cut and fold in the stiffly beaten whites of two eggs. Pour into well-greased and floured pan and bake in a moderate oven for forty minutes. Ice with butter cream icing.

HONEY CUSTARD

Place two cups of milk in a mixing bowl and add

Three-quarters cup of honey,
One-quarter teaspoon of nutmeg,
Two eggs.

Beat to thoroughly mix and then pour into custard cups. Place cups in a baking pan containing water and bake in a slow oven until firm in center.

HONEY RAISIN TAPIOCA

Wash one cup of tapioca well and then place in a saucepan and add

One cup of honey,
Four cups of water.

Bring to a boil and cook slowly until clear and the tapioca is soft, then add

One-half package of seeded raisins,
Yolk of one egg.

Stir to thoroughly blend and then cook fifteen minutes. Serve with fruit whip made of

One-half glass of jelly,
White of one egg.

Beat until the mixture holds its shape.

HONEY COOKIES

Place in a mixing bowl

Three-quarters cup of brown sugar,
Three-quarters cup of honey,
One egg,
Seven tablespoons of shortening.

Beat to blend and then add

Three and three-quarter cups of flour,

One-half cup of seeded raisins,
One-half cup of finely chopped nuts,
One teaspoon of baking powder,
One teaspoon of mace.

Roll and cut and then bake in a moderate oven for ten minutes.

HONEY CAKES

One cup of honey,
One-half cup of brown sugar,
One-half cup of shortening.

Cream well and then add

Yolks of three eggs,
Four cups of sifted flour,
One teaspoon of cinnamon,
One-half teaspoon of nutmeg,
One-half teaspoon of salt,
One and one-half teaspoons of baking soda, dissolved in,
One cup of sour milk.

Beat to thoroughly mix and then cut and fold in the stiffly beaten whites of three eggs. Pour into a well-greased and floured baking pan, about one inch deep. Bake in a moderate oven and cool. Cover with honey icing.

MALVERN CREAM

Place in a saucepan

Three-quarters cup of honey,
Two cups of milk,
Six level tablespoons of cornstarch.

Dissolve the starch in cold milk and honey and then place on the stove and bring to a boil. Cook for five minutes. Now add

One teaspoon of vanilla,
One-quarter teaspoon of nutmeg.

Beat to thoroughly mix and then rinse custard cups in cold water. Pour in the pudding and set aside to mould. When ready to serve unmould and serve with crushed fruit.

HONEY APPLE PUDDING

Two cups of stewed apples,
One cup of honey,
One-half cup of brown sugar,
Four tablespoons of shortening,
Two cups of fine bread crumbs,
One and one-half cups of flour,
Two level tablespoons of baking powder,
Two teaspoons of cinnamon,
One-half teaspoon of cloves.

Beat to mix and then put into a baking dish and bake in a slow oven for thirty-five minutes. Serve with a thin apple sauce, sweetened with honey.

HONEY AND RASPBERRY ADE

Place three baskets of well-washed raspberries in a saucepan and add

One quart of water,
One and one-half cups of honey,
One-quarter teaspoon of nutmeg.

Bring to a boil and cook slowly until the fruit is soft, mashing frequently with the potato masher. Cool and strain into punch bowl. Add a piece of ice and the juice of one orange or one lemon.

FATS

Fat is a heat-or fuel-producing food which is very valuable in cold weather for supplying the body with heat and energy. Often foods that are cooked in fat are termed indigestible; this means that the food is not utilized in the body and, owing to some digestive disturbances, it becomes part of the waste. Recent experiments tend to show that animal fats are assimilated fairly well; undoubtedly it is the misuse of fat that is used for frying purposes that has given many fried foods their bad reputation. Every normal person requires a certain amount of fat.

Make it a rule when serving fried food to have an acid food, either a vegetable or a garnish, accompany the dish.

Here are just a few things to keep in mind when planning to serve fried foods: Use very small quantities of foods that are cooked in fat for people occupying sedentary positions, while those who are employed in active or laborious work may eat a larger proportion. Persons who are working at hard manual labor, out of doors, will be able to assimilate daily portions of fried food without any physical disturbances.

For digestion's sake, learn to serve:

Juice of lemon with fried fish,
Apple sauce with pork or goose,
Cranberry or currant jelly with poultry, lamb or mutton,
Horseradish with beef.

It is a curious thing that nature demands these combinations to equalize the fatty content of the meal. Save and clarify the various fats and utilize each particular kind, so that there need be no waste. Chop all bits of suet fine and place in a double boiler and then render. Chicken and pork fat may be rendered in this way.

An excellent shortening that may be used to replace butter in cooking and baking may be made from chicken fat, of which there is usually three or more ounces in one fat bird. Remove the fat from the bird and place in cold salt water for one hour and then drain and cut into small pieces. Render in a double boiler. Pour into a jar and allow to harden. Now, when using this fat, use one-third less than the amount called for in the recipe. To make pastry, allow four tablespoonfuls of this chicken fat to each cup of flour. Chicken fat may be used to replace butter for seasoning vegetables and mashed potatoes. This is a pure fat free from moisture and seasoning and will go farther than butter.

Generally, in speaking of the term "drippings," it meant to include fats that cook out from the roast beef, pot roast, soups and corned beef. This fat is clarified and then used for sautéing. It cannot be used with good results for making pastry and cakes.

To clarify fat: Put the fat in a saucepan and add one cupful of cold water to every pound of fat. Add

One-fourth teaspoon of bicarbonate of soda,
One-half teaspoon of salt

Bring to a boil and then simmer slowly for ten minutes. Pour through a strainer lined with cheesecloth and allow to harden, then cut into pieces. Reheat and pour into jars. Bacon, sausage and ham fats may be blended with beef drippings for frying purposes.

Mutton or lamb fat must be clarified and then blended with ham and bacon or sausage fat. Fat from bacon, ham and sausages may be used for flavoring vegetables in place of butter, for cooking omelets, potato cakes, mush and scrapple. It is a splendid seasoning to use for macaroni, baked beans with tomato sauce, dried beans and peas in soups and when cooking dried lima beans. There is really no need to allow a spoonful of these fats to be wasted. Fats that are not available for table use should be collected and made into soap.

Do not be falsely economical in trying to do deep frying with these fats. They not only will not hold the temperature for successful frying without scorching, but they frequently soak into the food and make it unfit to eat.

The late war has brought many good vegetable oils upon the market that are ideal for cooking purposes and are preferable to the animal fats for all cooking. They not only hold a high temperature without burning, but also they may be used repeatedly if they are strained each time after using. Food cooked in vegetable oil does not absorb the fat and it is more digestible and really more economical.

FRYING

There are two methods of frying:

First.—Sautéing—cooking food in the pan with just sufficient fat to prevent scorching. This method is commonly used, but has nothing to really recommend it, as the food absorbs quantities of grease. This makes it difficult to digest.

Second.—Deep-fat frying—it is usual to dip the food to be fried in a mixture to coat it and then to roll it in fine bread crumbs and then cook in sufficient fat to cover. This forms an air-tight cover that prevents the grease from soaking through. A few essential utensils are necessary to produce successful results; first, a heavy kettle that will not tilt, and second, a frying basket, so that the food may be removed quickly when cooked.

The correct temperature for deep-fat frying is 350 degrees Fahrenheit, for raw foods, such as crullers, fish, fritters, potatoes, etc. For cooked dishes and oysters, cheeseballs, etc., 370 degrees Fahrenheit.

Do not attempt to cook large quantities at one time. This will cause a sudden drop in the temperature of the fat, allowing it to permeate the food which is cooking and thus give a greasy product.

Now for a word of protection. Do not use too large a kettle. Keep a bucket of sand handy in the kitchen, and if for any reason the fat catches fire, throw sand on it; do not attempt to remove it from the stove; serious burns are apt to result. Just turn out the light and throw sand on the fire. Keep the fact in mind that water spreads the flames; if no sand is at hand, use salt or flour.

MOCK CHERRY PIE

Pick over one and one-half cups of cranberries; then place in a saucepan and add

Three-quarters cup of raisins,
One cup of water.

Cook slowly until the berries are soft, and then cool. Now place

Three-quarters cup of sugar,
One-half cup of flour.

in a bowl and rub between the hands to mix. Add sugar and flour and stir until dissolved. Bring to a boil and cook for a few minutes. Cool. Bake between two crusts. This amount will make two pies.

CRANBERRY ROLL

Place in a bowl

Two cups of sifted flour,
One-half teaspoon of salt,
Four teaspoons of baking powder,
Six tablespoons of sugar.

Sift to mix and then rub in four tablespoons of shortening and mix to a dough with two-thirds cup of water or milk. Work to a smooth dough and then roll out one-quarter inch thick. Spread with a thick cranberry conserve; roll as for jelly-roll, tucking the ends in securely. Place in a well-greased baking pan and bake in a moderate oven for ten minutes. Start basting with

One-half cup of syrup,
Four tablespoons of water.

Serve the roll with cranberry sauce.

STRAWBERRY CUSTARD TART

This old English sweet is delicious. Line a pie tin with plain pastry and then cover the bottom of the prepared tin with strawberries. Then place in a bowl

One cup of milk,

Two eggs,
One-half cup of sugar.

Beat with egg-beater to thoroughly mix and then pour over the berries. Dust the top lightly with nutmeg and bake in a slow oven until the custard is firm. Set aside to cool. Dot the top with strawberry preserves.

CRANBERRY CONSERVE

Look over carefully and remove all the bruised and spoiled berries from one quart of cranberries. Place in a saucepan and add one cup of water. Cook slowly until soft and then rub through a sieve. Return to the saucepan and add

Two cups of sugar,
One cup of seeded raisins.

Bring to a boil and cook for ten minutes. Pour into a dish and set aside to cool.

CREAM PUFFS

Place one cup of water in a saucepan and add one-half cup of shortening. Bring to a boil and then add one and one-quarter cups of flour, stirring constantly. Cook until the mixture forms into a ball on the spoon, then lift into a bowl and now beat in three eggs, one at a time. Beat in each egg until well blended. Drop by the spoonful on well-greased baking sheet three inches apart. Bake for twenty minutes in a hot oven, then reduce the heat to moderate and bake for fifteen minutes longer. Do not open the oven door for ten minutes after putting the puffs in the oven.

PEACH ROLL

Place in a mixing bowl

Two cups of flour,
One teaspoon of salt,
Four teaspoons of baking powder,

Three tablespoons of sugar.

Sift to mix and then rub in five tablespoons of shortening, and mix to a dough with two-thirds of a cup of ice-cold water. Roll out on a well-floured pastry board one-quarter inch thick. Now cover with the prepared peaches and then sift over

One-half cup of sugar,
One-half teaspoon of cinnamon.

Roll as for jelly roll, tucking the ends in securely. Place in a well-greased and floured pan and bake in a moderate oven for forty-five minutes. Baste every ten minutes with

One-half cup of syrup,
Five tablespoons of water,
One-quarter teaspoon of nutmeg.

Stir to thoroughly mix before basting the roll. Remove the roll to a large platter when baked and serve cold, with crushed and sweetened peaches in place of a sauce.

To prepare the peaches for the roll select the fully ripe peaches and cut into thin slices; if they are clinging stones, cut into small pieces.

CHOCOLATE PIE

Place in a saucepan

One and one-half cups of water,
One-half cup of cocoa,
One-half cup of cornstarch,
One cup of sugar.

Stir until the cornstarch is dissolved and then bring to a boil and cook for five minutes. Cool and then pour into pastry lined pie tin. Bake in a slow oven for thirty minutes.

BUTTERSCOTCH PIE

Line a pie tin with plain pastry and then place in a saucepan

Three tablespoons of butter,
One cup of brown sugar.

Heat slowly and cook for three minutes. Then place one and one-half cups of cold milk in a bowl and add four level tablespoons of cornstarch to the milk. Stir to dissolve the starch and add to the cooked sugar and stir constantly to thoroughly blend. Bring to a boil and cook for three minutes. Cool and add

One well-beaten egg.

Then pour into the prepared pie plate. Care must be taken not to let the sugar caramel.

ARTICHOKES

The artichoke is a plant closely resembling the thistle, and it is extensively cultivated for its flowering head. The head is gathered just before the flower expands. The eatable portion is the fleshy part of the calyx, the bottom or basin of the blossom and the true base of the leaves of the flower.

The flesh of the artichokes correspond closely to that which the old world folks call the cheese of the thistle. On the Continent, in Europe, the artichoke is frequently served raw, as a salad, with either French or Parisian dressing. Under ordinary circumstances the fruit as prepared for market will keep several weeks. The canned artichoke, which was imported quite extensively before the war, consisted of the fronds and bottoms. It came in large quantities from both France and Italy.

The artichoke buds are used exclusively for garnishing.

THE JERUSALEM ARTICHOKE

This kind of artichoke is a tuber of the species of the sunflower; it resembles somewhat the Irish potato. It has a sweetish flavor and contains a large amount of natural water. This species of artichoke is more valuable than the common artichoke.

The two principal types of the Jerusalem artichokes are

First: Long with reddish skin,
Second: Round, knobby and white in color.

On the Continent they are frequently eaten raw, with just a plain seasoning of salt, pepper and vinegar; in fact, much as we eat the American radish. They are frequently made into soup.

The word Jerusalem is a queer cross of dialect from the Italian word *girasole*, meaning sunflower.

TO COOK

Soak the fruit in a bowl of cold water for two hours; then shake about in the water freely to remove all traces of sand. Plunge into boiling water and cook until tender; then drain. Serve in choice of following methods:

ARTICHOKE HOLLANDAISE SAUCE

Prepare artichoke as given above. Cut into pieces; then cook until tender; drain and lift each portion on a thin slice of toasted bread. Cover with Hollandaise dressing.

ARTICHOKE VINAIGRETTE

Cut one cold boiled artichoke into quarters; then place in deep bowl and cover with following dressing. Place in a bowl

One teaspoon of sugar,
One-half teaspoon of salt,
One-half teaspoon of paprika,
One-half teaspoon of mustard,

Juice of one-half lemon or two tablespoons of vinegar,
Five tablespoons of salad oil.

Beat to thoroughly mix. Now add one tablespoon of grated onion and stir until well blended. Place artichoke in nest of lettuce; pour over dressing. Serve garnished with finely chopped pimento.

ARTICHOKE FRIED IN BATTER

Cook artichoke until tender; drain and cut into eighths; dip in the batter; fry until golden brown in hot fat. Serve with cheese sauce.

Break in a bowl

One egg,
Two tablespoons of water,

Beat to mix. Add

Seven level tablespoons of flour,
One-half teaspoon of salt,
One-quarter teaspoon of pepper,
One teaspoon of vinegar,
One teaspoon of grated onion.

Beat well to mix; now dip artichoke in flour; then shake to loosen excess flour. Now dip in batter; fry golden brown.

ONIONS

ONION AND POTATO MINCE

Pare and slice sufficient onions to measure one cupful. Parboil and then drain. Now place four tablespoons of fat in a frying pan and add the onions and one and a half cups of mashed potatoes. Turn constantly until well blended and then form into an omelet shape in a pan, and turn on a warm platter and serve with cream sauce.

ONIONS IN RAMEKINS

Peel and boil until tender one dozen medium-sized onions. Drain and then place in ramekins. Season and cover with cream sauce. Dust the top with a few breadcrumbs and then sprinkle with one teaspoon of grated cheese. Dust lightly with paprika and then bake for fifteen minutes in a moderate oven.

ONIONS FRIED IN BUTTER

Pare and cook one dozen medium-sized onions until tender, taking care that they do not break. Drain and then cool, and when ready to prepare dip in batter and then fry in hot fat, and serve with Hollandaise sauce. How to prepare the batter:

Place in a bowl

Six tablespoons of water,
Eight tablespoons of flour,
One-half teaspoon of salt.

Beat to mix and then roll the onions in flour and then dip in a batter and fry until golden brown in hot fat.

FRENCH FRIED ONIONS

Peel large onions and then cut into one-half-inch slices. Fry until golden brown in hot fat and serve as a garnish with omelets, fish, cold meat, etc.

BAKED ONIONS

Large or Spanish onions are best for this dish. Peel the onions and then boil until tender, and then take care that the onion does not become soft. Lift and then cool, and carefully remove the centres. Now prepare the following as a filling for four large or eight medium-sized onions.

Four tablespoons of grated cheese,
Six tablespoons of fine bread crumbs,

One teaspoon of salt,
One teaspoon of paprika,
Two teaspoons of finely minced parsley,
One egg.

Mix thoroughly to blend and then fill the cavity of the onions, forming into a point or top one inch over the onion. Dust the onion lightly with flour and then place in a baking dish. Now baste onions with melted shortening and bake for twenty-five minutes in a moderate oven. Chop the onions which have been removed from the centres very fine and add to one cup of cream sauce with

One and one-half teaspoons of salt,
One-half teaspoon of white pepper,
Three tablespoons of parsley,
One well-beaten egg.

Beat to mix thoroughly and then heat to the boiling point. Serve over the baked onions. This dish will replace meat for luncheon.

SWISS ONION AND POTATO PANCAKES

Peel and put two Spanish onions through the food chopper, using a fine knife. Place in a bowl and then pare and grate four medium-sized potatoes into a bowl and add

Three-quarters cup of milk,
One egg,
One tablespoon of syrup,
One and one-half teaspoons of salt,
One-half teaspoon of pepper,
Seven-eighths cup of flour,
Two level teaspoons of baking powder,
Two level teaspoons of shortening.

Beat to mix and then fry like pancakes. Serve with parsley butter.

ONION CUSTARD

Chop sufficient onions to measure one-half cup. Parboil and then drain. Now place in a bowl

One and one-half cups of milk,
Two eggs,
One teaspoon of salt,
One teaspoon of paprika,
Two tablespoons of finely chopped parsley.

Beat to mix and then grease the custard cups. Add one-half cup of fine breadcrumbs to the prepared onions. Mix well and then divide into six cups. Pour the prepared custard on the top. Place the cups in a baking pan, add one quart of water and then place in a moderate oven and bake until firm in the centre, usually about twenty-five minutes. The water in the baking pan prevents the custards from cooking too fast. Serve in the cups or let stand for five minutes before taking from the mould and putting on a slice of toast.

PARSLEY BUTTER

Two tablespoons of butter,
Three tablespoons of finely minced parsley,
One teaspoon of lemon juice.

Beat to a smooth paste and use. This dish will replace potatoes in the luncheon menu.

HAVANA BANANA PASTRY

Two cups of flour,
One-half teaspoon of salt,
Two teaspoons of baking powder,
One tablespoon of sugar.

Place in a mixing bowl and sift to thoroughly mix. Now rub into the prepared flour eight tablespoons of shortening and then mix to a dough with one-half cup of ice-cold water. Roll the pastry on a slightly floured pastry board one-fourth inch thick; cut in oblongs three inches wide and six inches long. Peel the banana and lay on the pastry; sprinkle with

One teaspoon of brown sugar,
Pinch of nutmeg,
Pinch of cinnamon,
One-half teaspoon of butter.

Brush the edges of the pastry with cold water and press firmly together, inclosing the banana. Lay on a well-greased and floured baking sheet, placing the side which was fastened together down. Brush with beaten egg and bake in a moderate oven for eighteen minutes. Serve just as you would other pastries.

FRIED BANANAS

Peel the bananas and then cut into two; roll in flour and then dip in beaten egg and roll in fine crumbs. Fry until golden brown and serve with broiled steak or chops or chicken fricassee.

BANANA CUSTARD PIE

Pare and then rub through a fine sieve sufficient bananas to measure one cup. Place in a mixing bowl and add

One-half cup of sugar,
Juice of one lemon,
One-quarter teaspoon of grated rind of lemon.

Stir to mix and then add slowly, beating to mix

One cup of milk,
Yolk of one egg,
One whole egg,
One-quarter teaspoon of nutmeg.

Beat to mix and then pour in a pie plate lined with plain pastry. Bake in a slow oven for twenty-five minutes and then cool. Use the white of egg and one-half glass of jelly for fruit whip.

BANANA ICE CREAM

One and one-half cups of banana pulp,
One cup of sugar,
Juice of one lemon.

Place in a mixing bowl and then cover and set aside. Now place

Two and one-half cups of milk,
Four tablespoons of cornstarch,

in a saucepan and stir to dissolve the starch. Bring to a boil and cook for five minutes. Add the yolks of two eggs. Beat to thoroughly mix and add the banana mixture. Beat hard to blend. Now beat into the mixture the stiffly beaten whites of the two eggs. Freeze in the usual manner, using three parts ice to one part salt. This amount will make three pints of ice-cream.

BANANA STUFFING FOR CHICKEN

Pare and rub through a sieve four bananas. Place in a bowl and add

One-half grated onion,

One green pepper, chopped fine,
Three tablespoons of finely chopped parsley,
Four slices of bacon chopped fine,
One and one-quarter cups of bread crumbs,
Pinch of thyme,
One egg,
One teaspoon of salt.

Mix thoroughly and then fill into the chicken and roast in the usual manner.

BANANA FRITTERS

Place in a mixing bowl

One cup of banana pulp,
One-quarter cup of sugar,
Yolks of two eggs,
One tablespoon of shortening.

Beat to mix and then add

One and one-half cups of flour,
One and one-half teaspoons of baking powder.

Beat to mix and then cut and fold into the mixture whites of two eggs, beaten stiff. Fry in deep fat until golden brown and then serve with banana sauce.

BAKED BANANAS

Wash the bananas and remove just one strip from the top. Place in a baking pan and add one-half cup of water and bake in a moderate oven for one-half hour.

BANANA MUFFINS

Rub a sufficient number of bananas through a sieve to measure one cup. Place in a mixing bowl and add

One cup of brown sugar,
Four tablespoons of shortening,
Two cups of flour,
Five teaspoons of baking powder,
One cup of milk,
One-half teaspoon of nutmeg.

Beat to mix and then bake in well-greased and floured muffin pans in a moderate oven for twenty-five minutes. Ice the tops with water-icing.

RICE BANANAS AND POACHED EGGS

Cook one-fourth cup of rice in one and one-fourth cups of water until the rice is soft and the water absorbed. Place in a baking dish and cover one inch deep with sliced bananas. Place in the oven and bake for ten minutes. Now lay on one poached egg for each service. Garnish with a strip of bacon and serve with parsley sauce.

BANANA PANCAKES

Place in a mixing bowl

One cup of crushed bananas,
One cup of milk,
One and one-half cups of flour,
Two tablespoons of syrup,
Two tablespoons of shortening,
One egg,
Two teaspoons of baking powder.

Beat to mix and then bake in the usual manner on a well-greased smoking hot frying pan.

BANANA SAUCE

One-half cup of crushed banana,
One-half cup of sugar,
One teaspoon of vanilla,

Juice of one orange.

Beat to mix and then serve with the fritters.

FISH

Fish are divided into two classes—those having backbones, which are called vertebrates; and those which have no backbones, and are called shellfish.

The vertebrates are classified as fresh and salt-water fish, and they contain both white and dark meat. Fish is similar to meat in composition and structure and is classed among the protein or body-building foods; it may replace meat or its equivalent on the menu.

The muscle consists of a bundle of fibers, bound together by a connective tissue; it is so tender that it requires much less time to cook than meat. Fish, as a rule, contains less fat than meat, and while there is considerable refuse, it will be found to be about equal to the bone in meat.

The methods of cooking fish are: Broiling, boiling, baking, deep fat frying and sautéing.

TO BOIL FISH

Cleanse and prepare the fish. Tie in a piece of cheese-cloth and then plunge into a kettle of boiling court bouillon. Cook, allowing twenty minutes to the pound. Lift, drain well and then turn on a hot platter, laying a napkin under the fish to absorb the moisture. Serve with either cream, Hollandaise, egg or tomato sauce and garnish with slices of hard-boiled egg, beet and carrots cut in dice or capers, diced beets, slices of lemon.

BAKED FISH

Cleanse and prepare the fish, leaving the head and tail on the body, but remove the eyes and fins. Now prepare a filling as follows:

One cup of bread crumbs,

Three tablespoons of shortening,
One teaspoon of salt,
One teaspoon of paprika,
One small onion grated,
One egg.

Mix and then fill into the fish. Fasten the opening with a string or with toothpicks. Place in a baking dish and rub with plenty of shortening. Dust with flour and place in a hot oven to bake. Baste every fifteen minutes with boiling water. Allow eighteen minutes to the pound and twenty minutes for the fish to heat thoroughly and start baking.

COURT BOUILLON

Place five pints of water in a fish kettle and add

One small onion, sliced,
One clove,
Three branches of parsley,
One small red pepper,
One-half bay leaf,
One teaspoon of paprika,
One teaspoon of celery salt,
Two teaspoons of salt,
One-half cup of vinegar,
One fagot of soup herbs.

Bring to a boil and cook the fish. Strain and set aside to cook fish in again.

FISH SAUCE

Strain the liquid left in the pan after removing the fish and add sufficient boiling water to make one cup. Place in a saucepan and add

Two level tablespoons of cornstarch, dissolved in three level tablespoons of water,
One tablespoon of butter,
One tablespoon of Worcestershire sauce,

One teaspoon of salt,
One teaspoon of paprika,
Juice of one-half lemon.

Bring to a boil, cook for five minutes and serve with fish.

TO BROIL FISH

Cleanse the fish, leaving the small fish whole, split the large fish and then brush with melted shortening and broil, allowing ten minutes for small fish and ten minutes to the pound for larger ones.

Large fish will require thirty to forty-five minutes. Lift to a hot platter and spread with

Two tablespoons of butter,
Two tablespoons of parsley,
One tablespoon of Worcestershire sauce,
One tablespoon of lemon juice.

Mix well and then garnish with slices of lemon and parsley.

CREOLE FRIED FISH

The creole fried fish is a crisp golden brown. It is prepared as follows: Clean the fish and then wash and drain and roll it in flour. Place in a pan containing hot fat and fry until golden brown. Place in the oven, if the fish is large, until all is cooked and to finish cooking.

FRIED FISH

Small fish, like smelts, brook trout, perch, butter fish, etc., may be well cleaned, dried and then dipped in beaten egg and rolled in fine crumbs. Large fish should be cut into suitable pieces; sliced fish may also be prepared in this manner.

SAUTEING

Fish should be well cleaned and then fried in sufficient fat to prevent sticking.

COCOANUT PUDDING

Place in a mixing bowl

One cup of bread crumbs,
One cup of sifted flour,
One-half teaspoon of salt,
One tablespoon of baking powder,
Three-quarters cup of cocoanut,
One egg,
One cup of milk.

Beat to thoroughly mix and pour into well-greased custard cups or pudding pan and bake in a moderate oven for thirty-five minutes. Serve with lemon sauce.

SNOW PUDDING

Place in a saucepan

One cup of milk,
Four level tablespoons of cornstarch.

Stir to dissolve and then bring to a boil and cook slowly for five minutes. Now add

Six tablespoons of sugar,
Stiffly beaten white of one egg,
One teaspoon of vanilla.

Beat thoroughly to blend. Pour in four custard cups and set in a cool place to mould. Serve with custard sauce.

FRUIT PUDDING

Place in a bowl

One cup of molasses,

And add

One cup of sour milk,
One egg,
One teaspoon of baking soda,
Five tablespoons of shortening,
One teaspoon of cinnamon,
One-half teaspoon of allspice,
Four tablespoons of cocoa,
One and one-half cups of coarse bread crumbs,
One and one-half cups of wheat flour,
One-half cup of seeded raisins,
Two teaspoons of baking powder.

Mix in the order given, beating hard. Pour in well-greased and floured mould. Boil and steam for two hours and then serve with vanilla or cream sauce.

RICE PUDDING

Wash one-half cup of rice in plenty of cold water. Place in a saucepan and add three cups of boiling water. Cook slowly until water is absorbed and then grease a baking dish well. Pour rice in a bowl and add

Two cups of milk,
One yolk of egg,
One-half cup of sugar,
One-half teaspoon of nutmeg,
One-half teaspoon of salt.

Mix well and pour in a baking dish and bake in a slow oven for thirty-five minutes. Cook and then place the left-over white of egg and one-half glass of jelly in a bowl and beat until it will hold its shape. Use as a whip for the pudding.

CHOCOLATE RICE PUDDING

Wash one-half cup of rice in plenty of warm water and then place two and one-half cups of boiling water in a saucepan and add the rice. Cook until the rice is soft and the water absorbed. Now place three ounces of chocolate, cut into fine pieces, in one quart of milk. Bring to a boil and then add

Three-quarters cup of sugar,
One-half teaspoon of cinnamon extract,
Two teaspoons of vanilla,
Two tablespoons of butter,
The prepared rice.

Mix well and then pour into a baking dish and bake for forty minutes in a moderate oven. Stir frequently.

PLUM PUDDING, ROMANY STYLE

One cup of cooked oatmeal,
One cup of seedless raisins,
One cup of dried peaches, put through food chopper,
One cup of peanuts put through food chopper,
One-quarter cup of citron put through food chopper,
Two teaspoons of cinnamon,
One teaspoon of allspice,
One teaspoon of nutmeg,
One cup of syrup,
One egg,
One glass of jam or apple jelly.

Mix and then pack into moulds, one-pound coffee can or tie it in a pudding cloth. Boil for two hours.

BROWN BETTY

Pare the apples and then slice thin. Now grease a pudding mould or a baking dish. Place a layer one inch deep of apples, then layer of bread crumbs. Repeat until the dish is full and then sprinkle each layer with brown sugar and cinnamon, as it is placed. Now pour over the dish sufficient thick, well-sweetened apple sauce to fill the baking dish two-thirds full. Bake in a moderate oven for forty minutes.

LEMON PUDDING

Heat three-quarters cup of milk to the scalding point and then add

One tablespoon of butter,
Five tablespoons of sugar.

Pour over one-half cup of fine bread crumbs and then cool, and add

Yolk of one egg,
Juice of one-half lemon,
Grated rind of one-quarter lemon,
One-quarter cup of water.

Mix thoroughly before adding to the scalded bread crumbs. Pour into a small baking dish and bake in a moderate oven for twenty minutes.

Make a fruit whip of

One-half glass of apple jelly,
White of one egg.

Beat until mixture will hold its shape. Pile on pudding and brown in the oven for five minutes. Set aside to cool.

CRUMB COOKIES

One cup of molasses,
One-half cup of brown sugar,
Six tablespoons of shortening,
Two teaspoons of cinnamon,
One-half teaspoon of ginger,
One-half teaspoon of allspice,
One egg,

Five tablespoons of sour milk.

Beat to mix and then add

Two and one-half cups of coarse bread crumbs
and sufficient flour to make a very stiff mixture.

Drop by the spoonful on well-greased baking sheet, three inches apart. Bake in a moderate oven for ten minutes.

CARAMEL PUDDING

Make a caramel of

One cup of sugar,
Four tablespoons of water,
One tablespoon of butter.

Pour into a pudding dish and turn until the mixture thoroughly coats the dish. Now place in a mixing bowl

Three cups of apple sauce,
One cup of brown sugar,
Two cups of bread crumbs,
One-half cup of nutmeg.

Beat to mix and then pour into a baking dish, and bake in a slow oven for forty minutes, then turn out at once on a platter and serve with caramel sauce.

RAISIN PUDDING

Soak one-half cup of raisins in boiling water for one hour. Drain and then add two ounces of candied citron, and sufficient stale bread to make one cup of crumbs. Put all through the food chopper. Place in a bowl and add

One cup of brown sugar,
One cup of flour,

One tablespoon of baking powder,
Juice of one lemon,
Grated rind of one-half lemon,
Yolks of two eggs,
One cup of milk,
Three tablespoons of shortening.

Beat to thoroughly mix and then cut and fold in the stiffly beaten whites of two eggs. Pour into well-greased and floured one-quart mould. Place the mould deep in a pan containing sufficient boiling water to cover the mold two-thirds of its depth. Place in the oven and bake for fifty minutes in a moderate oven. Unmould and serve with Saboyon sauce.

PUMPKIN PUDDING

Place in a bowl

Eleven and one-half cups of steamed pumpkin drained dry,
One cup of milk,
Yolk of one egg,
One-half cup of sugar,
One teaspoon melted butter,
One teaspoon of cinnamon,
One-half teaspoon of nutmeg,
Two teaspoons of vanilla.

Beat thoroughly to mix and then pour into well-greased custard cups. Set cups in baking pan and pour in sufficient boiling water to half fill the pan. Bake in a moderate oven for forty-five minutes and then serve cold. Garnish with fruit whip or jelly.

SOUP

Soup, unless it is a thick cream or puree, contains little food value. Rather, it is stimulating to the stomach and causes a free flow of the digestive juices. Thus the food taken in after the soup has stimulated the stomach is quickly absorbed and thus gives the body immediate nourishment without distressing the digestion.

The French lay great stress upon two essentials in making soup successfully. First, it must not go below the boiling point, just a gentle bubbling, and, second, after once started, no water should be added. In making soup always use cold water to start with. Do not use salt or any seasoning, and heat slowly, keeping the pot closely covered.

Protein, which is the chief constituent of meat, is drawn into the liquid, making it very nutritious. Rapid boiling destroys the fine aroma and volatile oils, which escape in the steam.

Soups are divided into three classes: First, stock; second, cream; third, fruit soups.

Soups made from meat and bone are called stock; those without stock are called cream, such as cream vegetable, clam and oyster soups, and, lastly, those made from meat and bones, cooked by long and slow boiling, which dissolves the soluble elements of the meat and bones into the water and makes a very rich soup.

THE STOCK POT

This should be a deep pot or kettle with a tight-fitting lid. This is important, so that none of the steam may be lost by evaporation. The steam contains the aroma or fine volatile oil and essentials which pass into the air. In a fairly large family little meat need be purchased for the stock pot if the housewife insists that all portions of bone and trimming be sent with the purchased meat. The French women look with horror on the American women leaving all the scrap and trimming to the butcher.

TO MAKE THE STOCK

A soup bone from the shin, beef, which is full of nutriment, will have nearly one-half pound of meat on it. Take one pound of the scrag end of the neck of veal and four quarts of water. Wash the bones and add the cold water and bring slowly to a boil. Skim and then cover closely and cook for four hours.

By this time the meat will have fallen from the bones. Strain and set aside to cool. Let stand overnight. This is best.

Then remove all fat from the top. This stock is the basis of all soups, sauces and gravies. It is rich in mineral matter and gelatine. The meat can be taken from the bones and run through the food chopper and used for meat loaf, croquettes and meat biscuits or sausage, and it will make mighty tasty hash when combined with potatoes and onions for breakfast.

You now have a delicious and nutritious broth, without seasoning of any kind, which will keep in cold weather four or five days. In warm weather it must be returned every second day to the pot, brought to a boil and skimmed and then left to cool and finally put in the ice box. Small portions of meat, ham, any trimming and bones that have accumulated may be added. Chicken feet, scalded in boiling water to loosen the outer skin, which must be peeled off, together with the giblets of fowl, may be added to the stock pot. Seasoning and the addition of vegetables cause it to sour. Many varieties of soup are possible with the use of this stock.

OYSTER GUMBO

Mince two medium-sized onions very fine and then place in a saucepan and add

One pint of hot water,
One pint of oyster liquid,
One pint of milk.

Bring to a boil and cook for five minutes. Now add

One-half cup of flour dissolved in
One-half cup of milk.

Stir well until it reaches the boiling point, and then add

Twenty-five oysters,
One tablespoon of file (gumbo powder),
One ounce of butter.

Cook for five minutes and then pour the gumbo into a tureen and add three tablespoons of finely chopped parsley. File, or gumbo powder, is made by the Choxtaw Indians from young sassafras leaves. The Indians gather the leaves, spread them upon the bark to dry and then grind them into a fine powder, put it through a fine sieve and then pack it into pouches or jars. It is sold in the French markets in New Orleans and in all high-class importing groceries. The Indians use the sassafras both medicinally and in cookery, and the Creoles quickly discovered this and appreciated it when making their famous gumbo or file.

VEGETABLE SOUP

One pint of stock, one cup of tomato pulp, made by scalding the peeling of tomatoes, or the canned tomatoes, may be used, and

One-half cup of diced potatoes,
One-half cup of mixed vegetables; cabbage, turnips and peas, may be added
One-half carrot cut in dice,
One tablespoon of parsley,
Two tablespoons of flour,
Salt and pepper to taste,
Portion of bunch of potherbs.

Take a bunch of potherbs, divide into small bunches and tie each with a string and then use one of these in the vegetable soup. Put the remainder of the herbs in a fruit jar until needed again.

Put the herbs in the stock, add the tomatoes and let simmer. Cook the vegetables in one pint of water until tender and then add water and all to the stock and add the seasoning and flour, mixed with a little cold water, and cook for five minutes.

TO MAKE NOODLES

One egg,
One tablespoon of water,
One-half teaspoon of salt.

Beat together until well mixed and then add sufficient flour to make a stiff dough. Knead until elastic—about two minutes—and then roll out on a pastry board until as thin as paper, dusting the board lightly with flour to prevent sticking. Permit it to stand for fifteen minutes to dry and then cut into strings, thick and thin. Do this by rolling up loosely, like a jelly roll, and then cut. Lay on a dish to dry. When thoroughly dry they may be kept in a fruit jar. Part of the paste may be stamped with small vegetable cutters and cooked in the soup same as the noodles.

Vegetables cut in fancy shapes, macaroni cut in small rings, hard-boiled eggs in slices, cheese balls, slices of lemon, also rice and barley, may be added to the soup.

To make brown coloring: One-half cup of sugar cooked ten minutes in an iron pan until burned black; then add one-half cupful of water. Let come to a boil and then strain and bottle for use.

The principal points to keep in mind when making soup are:

First, draw out all of the juice and soluble flavors into the water.

Second, retain that which we have drawn out by using a pot with a tight-fitting lid.

Third, use cold water with which to extract meat juices and flavors.

Fourth, long, slow cooking.

Fifth, flavoring and vegetables added after making stock prevent its souring quickly.

Sixth, do not use stock pot for other than it is intended. Care and accurate judgment and measuring will give successful results.

If most of the work is done in the morning while attending to the kitchen duties, the stock-making will take little of your time. Delicious gravies may be made by using stock instead of water.

CLEAR SOUP

Use two tablespoons of fat and fry one onion until brown. Add two tablespoons of flour and brown well and then pour in one pint of stock and cook for five minutes, and then add seasoning, salt and pepper to taste. Strain into a soup tureen and sprinkle with one tablespoon of finely chopped parsley. Serve with bread cut in finger lengths and toasted.

CELERY PUREE

Use one pint of diced celery and cook in one cup of cold water until tender and then put through a sieve and add one cup of stock,

One cup of milk,
Two tablespoons of flour mixed with a little milk,
Seasoning,
Salt and pepper,
One tablespoon of chopped parsley and serve.

To the clear soup may be added macaroni, noodles or any vegetables. This is a good way to use left-over portions of vegetables that are too small to serve alone.

FISH SOUP

Use six slices of cod, hake or flounder. Mince four onions very fine and then place the onions in a saucepan with

Three tablespoons of cooking oil.

Cook until tender, but not brown; then add

One cup of tomatoes rubbed through a fine sieve,
One bunch of potherbs,
Three pints of water.

Bring to a boil and cook slowly for twenty minutes and then add the fish. Cook gently for thirty minutes and then add

Six tablespoons of flour dissolved in

One-half cup of water,
One and one-half teaspoons of salt,
One teaspoon of paprika,
Juice of one lemon,
Grated rind of one-quarter lemon.

Bring to a boil and cook for five minutes. Now lift the fish on slices of nicely toasted bread and strain over this the soup. Garnish with finely chopped parsley and one tablespoon of grated cheese.

FISH SOUPS

The bouillabaisse of France and New Orleans is most delectable and may well be served upon our tables frequently. The French and our Southern cooking, especially the creoles, excel in the preparation of delicious cream soups and purees. They are made entirely from vegetables. These good folk have preserved an old-world custom; namely, the daily plate of soup. The creoles have introduced a new variety of their own called gumbo.

Vegetables and milk are the basis for these soups. The vegetables are cooked in water and then rubbed through a sieve. Equal parts of milk are added and then thickened slightly and seasoned. When it is desired to give additional food value, eggs may be added.

OYSTER BROTH

Drain twenty-four oysters, saving the liquid. Wash and carefully look over the oysters to free from bits of shell. Chop fine and place in saucepan and measure the oyster liquid, adding sufficient water to make two cups. Simmer slowly for fifteen minutes. Let boil up once. Strain, season to taste with salt, pepper and then the broth is ready to serve. Equally good hot or cold.

PUREE OF OYSTER

Prepare two cups of thin cream sauce and add

Twenty-five oysters, chopped fine,

One and one-half cups of oyster liquid,
One tablespoon of grated onion.

Simmer slowly for twenty minutes and then bring to a scalding point. Strain, season to taste with salt and pepper, adding two tablespoons of finely minced parsley.

Clams may be used to replace the oysters.

TO PREPARE A STEW

Wash and look over the twenty-five stewing oysters carefully to free them from bits of shell. Place in small stewing pan and heat until the edges begin to curl. Then add

Three cups of scalding milk,
Two tablespoons of butter,
One teaspoon of salt,
One-half teaspoon of paprika.

Let the mixture come to the scalding point and then remove at once and serve.

Clams may be used to replace the oysters.

FISH SOUP

One red beet,
Three medium-sized onions,
One carrot,
Three leeks,
Six branches of parsley,
One and one-half cups of finely chopped cabbage.

Chop fine and then place in a saucepan and add two cups of cold water. Cook gently until the vegetables are very soft and then add

Three cups of fish stock.

Stock made by cooking the head, fins and bones of one and one-half pounds of fish. Season with

Two teaspoons of salt,
One teaspoon of paprika,
Juice of one-half lemon,
Two tablespoons of butter.

Simmer slowly for fifteen minutes and then place the prepared fish in a tureen and pour over the broth. Sprinkle with paprika and finely chopped parsley and then serve at once.

DEVILED CRABS

Make a cream sauce by placing in a saucepan

One cup of milk,
Five level tablespoons of flour.

Stir with a wire spoon or fork until the flour is dissolved in the milk and then bring to a boil. Stir constantly and cook for five minutes after it reaches the boiling point. Then add

One cup of crab meat,
One tablespoon of grated onion,
One tablespoon of finely minced parsley,
One tablespoon of Worcestershire sauce,
One and one-half teaspoons of salt,
One teaspoon of paprika,
One-half teaspoon of mustard.

Mix thoroughly and then fill into the crab shells, filling the shell slightly above the level. Dust lightly with flour and then brush with beaten egg and cover with fine bread crumbs. Fry until golden brown in hot fat. The crabs may be prepared earlier in the day and then reheated for serving.

CELERY SOUP

Wash and thoroughly cleanse the celery and then chop fine. Place one pint of finely chopped celery in a saucepan and add three cups of cold water. Bring to a boil and cook until the celery is very soft. Rub through a fine sieve and then measure, and add

One cup of milk,
Two tablespoons of flour.

to every cup of the celery puree. Dissolve the flour in cold milk and then add the celery puree. Bring to a boil and cook for ten minutes. Season, adding one teaspoon of butter for flavoring. A faggot of soup herbs may be added to the celery if desired.

CREAM SOUPS

Cream soups are a combination of vegetables, puree and milk. Almost all of the green vegetables will make delicious soups. Clean the vegetables well and then cut into small pieces. Place in a saucepan and cover with cold water and bring to a boil. Cook slowly until tender and then mash well; then rub through a fine sieve. Use this vegetable stock with equal parts of milk to make the soup.

Carrots, peas, tomatoes, turnips, corn, beans, celery, lettuce, potatoes, beets, cucumbers, asparagus, all these afford a splendid variety.

Allow one level tablespoon of flour for thickening and dissolve the flour in cold water before adding. Bring quickly to a boil and then season. Add two tablespoons of butter for flavoring and then serve.

French, Swiss and Italians serve grated cheese and paprika with all cream soups.

CREAM OF ONION

Place two cups of thinly sliced onions in a saucepan and add one cup of cold water. Cook until soft and then rub through a fine sieve. Measure and return to the saucepan, and add one cup of milk for every cup of onion puree and two level tablespoons of flour to every cup of milk. Stir to dissolve the flour, then bring to a boil and cook slowly for five minutes. Season, using salt and white pepper. Serve, then add one tablespoon of butter to every quart of cream soup. Croutons or toasted strips of bread make a delicious accompaniment to cream soups.

How to prepare croutons: Cut slices of bread into one-inch blocks and place in a baking sheet and bake until golden brown. Place in a tin box or jar and seal. When ready to use just reheat to crisp and then serve. Stale bread may be used for this purpose.

CREAM OF TOMATO

Place two cups of stewed tomatoes in a saucepan and add

One onion, chopped fine,
One faggot of soup herbs,
Pinch of cloves.

Cook gently for ten minutes and then run through a fine sieve. Now place in a saucepan

Two cups of milk,
Five tablespoons of cornstarch.

Stir until dissolved and then bring to a boil and cook for five minutes. Add to prepared tomato, beating well to thoroughly mix. Now add

One teaspoon of salt,
One-half teaspoon of pepper,
One tablespoon of butter.

The making of the cream sauce and then adding the prepared tomato prevents curdling.

TOMATO PUREE

One pint of stewed tomatoes,
Two onions chopped fine,

One carrot cut in dice,
One faggot of soup herbs,
One pint of water.

Cook slowly until the vegetables are soft, rub through a sieve and then dissolve

Four tablespoons of cornstarch in
Five tablespoons of cold water.

Add to the tomato sauce mixture with

Two tablespoons of butter,
One and one-half teaspoons of salt,
One-half teaspoon of pepper.

Cook slowly for ten minutes.

VEGETABLE PUREE

Pare and cut in dice

Six medium-sized turnips,
Four medium-sized carrots,
Six medium-sized onions.

Chop fine

One small head of cabbage,
Four branches of celery,
One bunch of potherbs,
One teaspoon of thyme.

Place in a saucepan and add seven pints of cold water. Bring to a boil and cook slowly for two hours. Mash through a fine sieve and then return to the kettle and add

One-half cup of flour dissolved in

One cup of milk,
One and one-half tablespoons of salt,
One teaspoon of pepper,
Two well-beaten eggs,
Butter, size of large walnut or one ounce.

Stir to thoroughly blend and then add one-quarter cup of finely chopped parsley. Serve with toast.

CABBAGE SOUP

Two quarts of water,
Three onions, chopped fine,
One faggot of soup herbs,
Two slices of salt pork, cut into dice,
One and one-quarter pounds of soup meat, with bone in it,
Two and one-half cups of finely shredded cabbage.

Place in a saucepan and cook slowly for one and three-quarter hours. Now add two tablespoons of flour, dissolved in one-quarter cup of water, and season with

One tablespoon of salt,
One teaspoon of pepper,
One-half teaspoon of thyme.

CREAM OF CUCUMBER

Pare and grate one large cucumber, and then place in a saucepan and add

One cup of cold water,
One tablespoon of grated onion.

Bring to a boil and cook slowly for ten minutes. Rub through a fine sieve and add

Four cups of milk,
Six tablespoons of flour.

Stir to dissolve the flour, and then bring to a boil and cook slowly for five minutes. Now add

One teaspoon of salt,
One-half teaspoon of paprika,
One quarter green pepper, chopped fine,
One tablespoon of butter,

Beat hard to mix.

CREAM OF CORN, SUPREME

Use a corn scraper and then score and scrape the pulp from four large ears of corn, and rub through a sieve into a saucepan. Now add

Four cups of milk,
Six tablespoons of flour,
One tablespoon of grated onion.

Stir to dissolve and then bring to a boil and cook slowly for five minutes. Season to taste and add

One tablespoon of butter,
One tablespoon of finely minced parsley.

BAKED PRUNES

Wash and soak the prunes and then place in a casserole dish and add one-half pound of fruit,

Paring of lemon rind,
Juice of one-half lemon,
Four tablespoons of brown sugar and just barely enough of water to cover.

Bake for thirty minutes.

FRUITS

BAKED PEARS

Select pears of uniform size and then pare and cut in half. Place in a baking dish and add

One-half cup of syrup,
One-half cup of water,
One-quarter teaspoon of nutmeg.

Bake until pears are tender. Baste frequently with the syrup.

PEAR TARTS

Line pie tins or tart pans with plain pastry. Fill with stewed pears and then dust with cinnamon and bake in a slow oven. Top with fruit whip.

PEAR BREAD PUDDING

Place a layer of broken stale bread in the bottom of a well-greased pudding pan and then a layer of thinly-sliced pears. Season each layer of bread and pears slightly with nutmeg and cinnamon. When the dish is full pour over

One cup of syrup,
One-half cup of brown sugar,
One cup of water.

Stir until sugar is dissolved and then bake in a slow oven for one hour. Serve with custard sauce.

PEAR SAUCE

Pare and then cover with just enough water to cook. Cook until tender and then mash and put through a fine sieve or colander. Sweeten to taste, adding

Juice of one lemon.

One tablespoon of either cinnamon or nutmeg to each quart of the pear sauce. This may be used and served with roast duck, chicken, or as a side dish, and in pear shortcake and as a spread for bread and hot cakes.

BAKED PEARS AND CRANBERRIES

Pare eight pears and then cut in half, removing stems and seeds. Place in a baking dish with the cut side up. Sort over and wash one cup of cranberries and then add the berries to the pears and

One-half cup of raisins,
One cup of syrup,
One-half cup of brown sugar,
One cup of water,
One-quarter teaspoon of nutmeg.

Bake in a slow oven until the pears are soft.

NOTE.—This dish may be cooked upon the top of the stove in a saucepan.

DRIED FRUIT

Oranges and grapefruit are high-priced and the dried fruits may be substituted to advantage. If these fruits are nicely prepared, the family will hardly be able to distinguish between them and the fresh fruit.

Frequently the dried fruits are so prepared that they are anything but inviting. Much will depend upon the selection of these fruits. Purchase only the best grade. This fruit should be bright and waxy and not too dry. Soak for fifteen minutes in warm water; this loosens the dirt before washing. Now wash in plenty of water. Cover with water and allow to stand until the fruit has plumped out; each piece of fruit will only absorb just the amount of moisture as it originally contained.

This will require from six to twelve hours, depending entirely upon the dryness of the fruit. Be sure that the water covers the fruit at least one inch. Now, when the fruit is ready, add sugar to sweeten and place in the stove to cook. The slower this fruit is cooked the better. Remember that hard, rapid cooking not only spoils dried fruits, but fresh fruit as well.

When cooked tender, drain the liquid from the fruit and measure. Allow one-half cup of sugar to every three cups of juice. Place this juice and the sugar in a separate saucepan and boil until thick; then pour over the fruit.

Dried fruits prepared this way will be found to be delicious. Apricots will require very little cooking, so drain them free from the liquid in which they are soaked and add the sugar. Boil the syrup until thick and then pour over the apricots and cook gently for ten minutes.

Remove the skins from peaches, after soaking them, and before cooking add a little piece of thin orange peel for flavor.

To prepare dried pears soak them for twelve hours and then place in a casserole dish and add to one-half pound of fruit

One cup of brown sugar.
Juice of one lemon,
One cup of raisins.

Cover the casserole dish and bake slowly.

STEWED PEARS

Three-quarters cup of syrup,
One-half cup of water,
Six cloves,

Piece of cinnamon and piece of lemon peel,

Peel and then cook slowly until tender, chill and serve.

CHICKEN AND GREEN PEPPER SANDWICHES

Remove the seeds from two green peppers and add one small onion and chop very fine. Mince one cup of chicken meat fine and add to the green peppers and onions and then season with

One teaspoon of salt,
One-quarter teaspoon of mustard,
One-half teaspoon of paprika,
Two tablespoons of melted butter.

Mix well and then spread between thin slices of buttered bread.

BROILED CHICKEN, VIRGINIA STYLE

Select a plump broiler, weighing from one and a half to two pounds. Singe and then split with a sharp knife down the back. Draw. Remove the head and feet and then wash and parboil for eight minutes. Now flatten well with a rolling pin. Rub with shortening and broil for ten minutes. Garnish with bacon. Bacon or ham fat will give the bird a delicious flavor.

CHICKEN A LA KING

Cut the breast of cooked chicken into one-inch pieces and then place one and a half cups of thick sauce in a saucepan and add one cup of mushrooms that have been peeled and cut in pieces and then parboiled for six minutes in boiling water, and also

One green pepper, diced fine and parboiled,

Add

Yolks of two eggs,
Juice of one-half lemon,

One-quarter teaspoon of mustard,
One and one-half teaspoons of salt,
One teaspoon of paprika,

in the cream sauce. Also add the prepared chicken, the mushrooms and then green pepper. Heat until the boiling point is reached and then simmer slowly for ten minutes and serve on toast.

BREAST OF GUINEA HEN, TERRAPIN STYLE

Cut the breasts of two cooked guinea hens into one-inch blocks and place in a chafing dish and add

Three cups of thick cream sauce,
One well-beaten egg,
One-half teaspoon of mustard,
One teaspoon of salt,
One teaspoon of paprika,
One large onion chopped very fine,
Three tablespoons of finely chopped parsley,
Juice of one large lemon,
Grated rind of one-half lemon.

Stir to mix thoroughly and add the prepared breasts of the guinea hens and heat slowly until very hot. Serve on toasted waffles.

GUINEA HEN—POT PIE

Draw and singe the pair of guinea hens, removing the wings, thighs and legs and leaving the breast whole. Break the back of the carcass and then place in a deep saucepan and add seven cups of boiling water and steam slowly until tender. Add

A piece of carrot,
One small onion,
One branch of celery

for flavoring and then lift and set the thighs and breast aside for future use. Pick the meat from the back of the carcass and add to two and one-half cups of the stock. Season and thicken slightly. Now place the legs and wings in a casserole dish and add

One cup of peas,
The prepared gravy,
Four boiled onions.

Cover with a crust of plain pastry and bake in a moderate oven for thirty minutes.

FRICASSEE CHICKEN

Draw and singe and cut the chicken. Wash and place in a deep saucepan and cover with boiling water. Bring to a boil and add

One onion,
One small carrot,
Two branches of celery.

Cook slowly until tender and then thicken the gravy. Dumplings may be added if desired.

ROAST CHICKEN, SPLIT STYLE

Prepare the chicken as for roasting. Do not fill. Rub well with shortening and then pat in plenty of flour. Place in a roasting pan and roast until tender; baste frequently with hot water.

ROAST DUCK

Singe and draw the duck and then remove the neck and add to the giblets and cook until tender. Wash and then drain the duck. Now prepare a filling by soaking sufficient stale bread in cold water. When pressed dry it will measure two and one-half cups. Rub through a sieve. Now place five tablespoons of shortening in a saucepan and add

One cup of chopped onion,
One green pepper, chopped fine,
The prepared bread,
Three tablespoons of finely chopped parsley,
One level teaspoon of thyme.

Cook slowly, turning frequently until the onions are tender, adding more shortening if necessary to prevent the mixture from sticking to the pan. Then season with salt and pepper. Cook and then fill into the duck. Dust with flour and then roast in a moderate oven, allowing thirty minutes for the duck to start cooking and twenty minutes to the pound.

MACARONI

Macaroni is to the Italian cook the starchy content of the meal; just as the Irish and sweet potato are our common starchy foods. The thrifty Italian and French housewifes have found that by addition of meat, cheese and eggs for flavoring, they can serve their families substantial and attractive foods at a minimum cost.

The average American consumer of pastes and macaroni has no idea of the number of styles or forms—of which there are over a hundred—into which this wheat product is made. They range from the lasagnes, which are the short, flat pieces one and two inches wide, cut and frequently moulded by hand, to the fideline, which are the long, thin threads, the finest of which are many times smaller than vermicelli. Between these two extremes there is a great variety, which includes the alphabet and many fancy designs.

MACARONI MILIEUSE

Wipe with damp cloth and cut in one-inch blocks one pound of shin beef. Roll in flour and brown quickly in hot fat. Place in a deep saucepan and add

Three pints of cold water,
Two onions cut fine,
One medium-sized carrot cut in dice.

Bring to a boil and cook gently until the meat is tender. Now add

One-half cup of tomato aux fines herbes,
Two teaspoons of salt,
One and one-half teaspoons of paprika,
Six ounces of prepared macaroni.

Bring this mixture to a boil and then cook until the macaroni is well heated. Pour on a large platter and garnish with finely chopped parsley.

TO PREPARE MACARONI

The macaroni may be broken into pieces one and one-half inches long, or it may be cooked whole. In all recipes the macaroni must first be prepared as follows:

Grease the bottom of a deep saucepan and then add two quarts of boiling water. Let boil for two minutes and then add the macaroni. Stir for a few minutes and then cook for fifteen minutes. Turn into a colander and drain. Then blanch under the running cold water for three minutes. Let drain. It is now ready to use in any number of ways. Greasing the saucepan prevents the macaroni from sticking to the bottom, while it is cooking.

The Italian prepares a seasoning as follows:

Wash two leeks,
Six branches of parsley,
Two green or red peppers,
Four branches of celery.

Pare

Six onions,
Tiny bit of garlic.

Place in a chopping bowl and chop very fine. Now place in one-half cup of vegetable cooking oil in a saucepan and add the vegetables. Cook slowly until soft and then add one small can of tomato paste. Blend well and then pour in a bowl or jar and set in a cool place. This mixture will keep in the refrigerator or in a cool place for one week in summer time and from ten to twelve days in winter. This mixture is called tomato aux fine herbes.

Small portions of meat that would be insufficient to serve alone can be utilized in making these dishes. When making gravy, prepare enough so that a cup or more may be set aside to use in the macaroni dishes. Bones, gristle and meat joints left on the serving platter may all be made into stock, from which the various gravies can be made. The Italian cook uses a small piece of meat for flavoring, usually chopping it in small pieces.

MACARONI CUSTARD

Place in a saucepan

Two cups of milk,
One and one-half cups of water,
Six level tablespoons of cornstarch.

Dissolve the starch in the water and add the milk. Bring to a boil and cook for five minutes. Remove from the fire and add

Yolks of two eggs,
One cup of sugar,
One and one-half teaspoons of vanilla.

Beat to mix and then pour over six ounces of macaroni prepared as given in the method for preparation. Add one-half cup of raisins and then bake in a moderate oven for twenty-five minutes. Place the whites of two eggs in a bowl and add one glass of jelly. Beat until the mixture holds its shape; then pile on top of pudding.

MACARONI AU GRATIN

Cook one-half pound of macaroni as given in the method of preparing. Place in a baking dish and then make three cups of cream sauce, using

One and one-half cups of milk,
One and one-half cups of clear stock,

One-half cup of flour.

Blend well and then pour over the macaroni. Sprinkle the top with fine bread crumbs and grated cheese and bake in a moderate oven for twenty-five minutes.

POTATOES

This nutritious tuber is said to have saved the Irish people from famine, and it is fitting that this variety of potato should bear that name. The potato was unknown to Europe before the venturesome expedition of the fifteenth century to the Americas, where it was found to be used freely by the natives of both continents.

Frequently it has been said that the potato competes with bread as the staff of life, because its use is almost universal. There are more than thirty-five varieties of potato and although it is affected by soil and climate, the sandy soil necessary for its successful growth is found in almost every country.

The housewife should understand its food value. The average analysis of the white potato is as follows:

Sixty-two per cent. water, 2 per cent. protein, 1 per cent. fat, 4 per cent. carbohydrates (starch and sugar), 20 per cent. waste and 1 per cent. mineral ash.

The proportion of water found in the potato depends largely upon the soil in which it is grown. The small protein content is offset by its large carbohydrates (starch and sugar) content.

POTATO CAKES

Cook three large potatoes and then peel and mash fine. Measure and place two cups of mashed potatoes in a mixing bowl and add

Two cups of flour,
One teaspoon of salt,
Four teaspoons of baking powder,

One egg,
Four tablespoons of milk.

Mix to a smooth dough and then roll out one-half inch thick and cut and brush the tops with milk. Bake in a hot oven for eighteen minutes.

POTATO DISHES

One of the best forms of serving this tuber is to roast the potato in the ashes. Few will realize how delicious it can be. Wrap the potato in wax paper and then cover with coals and roast about one hour.

Next to this method comes the baked potato. Wash and dry medium-sized potatoes and then rub well with shortening and place in the oven and bake for thirty-five minutes for small potatoes and fifty minutes to one hour for large ones. Greasing the potato well before baking prevents a hard crust from forming and permits the entire contents of the mealy sack to be eaten. Boiling potatoes in their jackets causes the potato to lose about 2 per cent. of its nutritive value, while peeling before cooking causes a loss of 14 per cent. If necessary to peel, use a sharp knife and removed the very thinnest portion of the skin; scraping new potatoes is better than peeling them.

O'BRIEN POTATOES

Pare and then cut in thin slices five potatoes that have been boiled in their jackets. Mince sufficient onions, fine, to measure three-quarters of a cup. Chop fine two green peppers. Parboil onions and peppers until tender and then drain well. Now heat three tablespoons of shortening in a frying pan until very hot and then add the potatoes and let brown. Fold over and brown again. Keep turning over until the potatoes are well browned and then add the prepared onions and peppers. Cook slowly for five minutes and then turn on a hot platter and garnish with finely chopped parsley.

BOILED POTATOES

To cook potatoes, either in jackets or pared: Cover with boiling water, cook until tender. Season; now cover closely with clean cloth to absorb moisture and the potato will be mealy.

GRILLED POTATOES

Wash and pare large old potatoes and then cut into thin slices, cutting the full width of the potato. This means that you are to cut a thin slice of raw potato that will cover your hand. Place on a shallow baking dish and brush with shortening. Place in the broiler and broil until nicely browned, then place in the oven for five minutes.

MOUNTAIN BUTTERMILK RYE MUFFINS

Place in a mixing bowl

One and one-half cups of buttermilk,
One teaspoon of baking soda,
Four tablespoons of shortening,
Six tablespoons of syrup,
One egg.

Beat to mix and then add

Two and one-half cups of rye flour,
One teaspoon of baking powder.

Beat to thoroughly mix and then pour into well-greased and floured muffin pans, and bake for thirty minutes in a moderate oven. When cold the muffins that are left over may be split and toasted and then spread with mountain sweet-spiced jam.

IF NECESSARY TO KEEP MEAT THREE OR FOUR DAYS

Much sickness that is described as ptomaine poisoning is usually caused by carelessness. If for any reason meat must be kept several days after it is purchased, it may be cared for in the following manner:

Place

Three-quarters cup of salt in a saucepan

And add

Three and one-half cups of water,
One bay leaf,
One-half teaspoon of saltpeter.

Bring to a boil and cool. Place the meat in a china bowl or a wooden bucket and pour the brine over it. Now place a plate on top of the meat and weigh down with an old flatiron and heavy stone. Turn the meat every other day.

This meat will keep for one week. This method is suitable for mutton, beef or pork. For lamb or chicken place in a saucepan and add

One-half carrot,
One onion,
Sufficient boiling water to partially cover same.

Cook, keeping pan closely covered, for ten minutes to the pound. Cool before placing in the ice box. If it is necessary to keep the meat only until the next day, mince fine two onions and add

Four tablespoons of salt,
One tablespoon of pepper.

Mix thoroughly and then rub the meat thoroughly with this mixture. Meat may be kept in the ordinary ice box that holds seventy-five pounds of ice for two days in the hottest weather in the following manner: Wipe the meat with a dry cloth and cover with a wax or parchment paper, and then hang from a hook in the lower part of the refrigerator, directly under the ice chamber if possible. The hooks are shaped like the letter S, sharply pointed at both ends and they may be purchased or made by any hardware dealer.

Meat allowed to lie on a platter soon loses its nutritious qualities with the escaping of the juices.

FILLET OF BEEF

Have the butcher trim the fillet into shape and then lard it with salt pork. Dust lightly with flour and then place on a rack in the roasting pan and place in a hot oven, basting every ten minutes. Cook, allowing the meat one-half hour to become thoroughly heated and to start cooking; then allow twelve minutes for every pound. This cut is the choicest of the entire cattle and is without a single ounce of waste. It is delicious either hot or cold.

WELSH CHEESE PUDDING

Five ounces of grated cheese,
One cup of bread crumbs,
One cup of flour,
One and one-half teaspoons of salt,
One teaspoon of white pepper,
One teaspoon of paprika,
One tablespoon of Worcestershire sauce,
One tablespoon of baking powder,
Four tablespoons of grated onions,
One egg,
One cup of milk.

Beat to thoroughly mix and then pour in moulds or prepared pudding cloth and boil for one and three-quarters hours. Serve either hot or cold. To serve hot, use the following sauce:

Place in a saucepan

One cup of milk,
Two tablespoons of cornstarch.

Dissolve the starch in the milk and bring to a boil. Cook for five minutes and then add

One well-beaten egg,
One teaspoon of salt,
Two teaspoons of paprika,
Juice of one-half lemon.

Beat hard to mix and then serve. This dish will replace meat and be sufficient for a family of four or five.

MEAL PUDDING

Place one quart of milk in a saucepan and bring to a boil; then add three-quarters cup of fine cornmeal. Stir until thick, and cook slowly for ten minutes and then add

One cup of sweet spiced jam,
One cup of syrup,
One-half cup of sugar,
One-half teaspoon of nutmeg.

Beat to mix and then pour into a baking pan and bake slowly for three-quarters of an hour. Cool and then serve with plain cream.

HOW TO COOK CORN BEEF

Wash the beef in cold water and then place in a saucepan and cover with cold water. Bring to a boil and turn into a colander, and let cold water run on the meat. Place a saucepan on the stove and fill with boiling water, and add

One carrot, cut in dice,
Two onions, with one clove stuck in each onion,
One bay leaf and,
The meat.

Bring to a boil and cook slowly, allowing the meat to cook thirty minutes to start and then twenty minutes to the pound, gross weight. Then remove the saucepan from the fire when the meat is cooked and allow the meat to cool in the liquid, with the lid removed. When cool, remove and place at once in the ice box. Serve cold.

Mutton may be corned like beef. The shoulder makes a delicious economical cut. Have the butcher bone the meat, but do not roll. Put in a pickle for six days. Remove and wash and then tie securely, and cook in the same manner as for corned beef.

OLD PHILADELPHIA STEWED KIDNEY

Wash and dry the kidney and cut into inch pieces; put on to boil in a pot of cold water; as soon as boiling point is reached, remove from the fire, turn in colander and drain, rinse in cold water and dry. Dust lightly with flour; put three tablespoons of shortening in a pot; when hot toss in the kidney, browning carefully; then add two cups of water, which must be boiling, and cook until the kidney is tender. Then season with salt and pepper, five tablespoons of catsup, three tablespoons of vinegar; add one tablespoon each of grated onion and fine chopped parsley. Serve on toast for breakfast.

MEAT PUDDINGS

Put sufficient cold meat through the chopper to measure three-quarters of a cup. Place in a mixing bowl and add

One cup of cold boiled rice,
One small onion, grated,
One green pepper, chopped fine,
Two teaspoons of salt,
One teaspoon of paprika,
Two teaspoons of garlic vinegar,
One-half teaspoon of thyme,
One egg,
Five tablespoons of cold stock, water or gravy.

Mix thoroughly and then grease and flour the custard cups and fill a little better than just one-half full. Spread the top smoothly and place in a pan containing water, and then bake for forty minutes in a moderate oven. Unmould and cover with either cream or brown sauce.

CORN PUDDING

Place in a mixing bowl

One can of crushed corn,
One cup of prepared bread,
Two eggs,
One-half cup of milk,
One onion, grated,
Four tablespoons of finely minced parsley,
Two teaspoons of salt,
One teaspoon of paprika.

Mix well and then pour in the prepared custard cups. Set cups in a pan of warm water and bake for thirty-five minutes in a moderate oven.

To prepare the bread:

Soak the stale bread in hot water and place in cloth and squeeze dry.

To prepare the cups:

Grease well and then dust with bread crumbs.

SALT CHOWDER

Mince fine four ounces of salt pork or bacon. Place in a deep kettle and add

One cup of chopped onions,
One-half cup of chopped sweet red peppers,
One cup of chopped tomatoes.

Cook slowly for ten minutes and then add one pound of fish, bones and skin removed, fish cut in one-inch blocks.

Six large clams cut in pieces,
Two cups of water.

Cover closely and then boil for twenty minutes. Now add

One teaspoon of sweet marjoram,
One-quarter teaspoon of thyme,

Two and one-half cups of cream sauce,
One cup of cooked peas,
One cup of cooked lima beans,
One-half cup finely chopped parsley,
Two tablespoons of butter,
One tablespoon of salt,
One and one-half teaspoons of pepper.

Heat until scalding and then serve.

STEAMED SALT OYSTERS OR CLAMS

Place the salt oysters or clams in a large dishpan and cover with plenty of cold water. Scrub clean with a stiff brush. Now place a colander in a deep scaucepan and add one quart of boiling water. Fill the colander with salt oysters or clams and steam until they open their mouths. Place one dozen of the steamed salt oysters or clams in a deep soup plate and serve with a small saucer of melted butter. Serve a small cup of the salt oyster or clam liquid, left in the saucepan after steaming the bivalves, with them.

CLAM FRITTERS—RED RIVER BOATHOUSE STYLE

Mince one dozen large clams fine and then drain free of the liquid. Measure the liquid and add sufficient milk to measure one and one-half cups. Place in a bowl and add

One egg,
Two teaspoons of salt,
One teaspoon of paprika,
Two tablespoons of grated onion,
Four tablespoons of finely chopped parsley,
One tablespoon of shortening,
One teaspoon of sugar,
The minced clams,
Two cups of sifted flour,
Four level teaspoons of baking powder.

Beat hard and then fry in very hot fat in shallow pan.

DEVILED CLAMS

Place in a saucepan

One-half cup of clam juice,
One-half cup of milk,
Five tablespoons of flour.

Stir to dissolve and then bring to a boil and cook for five minutes. Now add

Six clams minced fine,
One tablespoon of grated onion,
Four tablespoons of finely minced parsley,
One-quarter teaspoon of mustard,
One-half teaspoon of paprika,
One teaspoon of salt,
Six tablespoons of bread crumbs.

Mix thoroughly and then fill into well-cleaned clam shells, rounding up on top. Dust with flour and then coat with beaten egg and then cover, patting well, with fine crumbs. Fry until golden brown in hot fat.

CLAM FRITTERS

Mince six clams fine and then place in a bowl and add sufficient milk to the clam juice to make one and one-half cups. Pour over minced clams and add

Two and one-quarter cups of flour,
One and one-half teaspoons of salt,
One-half teaspoon of pepper,
One well-beaten egg,
Two tablespoons of baking powder (level),
One tablespoon of grated onion,
Three tablespoons of finely minced parsley.

Beat to a smooth batter and then fry in deep fat.

CLAM COCKTAIL

Use four cherrystone clams for each service. Prepare a cocktail sauce as follows:

One cup of canned tomatoes,
One leek, chopped fine,
One onion, chopped fine,
Pinch of thyme,
Pinch of cloves,
One-half teaspoon of mustard,
One-half cup of water.

Cook for fifteen minutes, cool and then rub through a sieve and add

One and one-half teaspoons of salt,
One teaspoon of paprika,
One tablespoon of Worcestershire sauce.

Mix and then divide into four portions.

CLAMS

Clams may be served and cooked in a manner similar to oysters.

BAKED HAM

Place a four and one-half to five-pound cut from the butt end of the ham in the fireless cooker overnight. In the morning remove the skin and then pat into the fat part of the ham

Five tablespoons of brown sugar,
One teaspoon of cinnamon,
Three-quarters teaspoon of allspice.

Place in a hot oven and bake for forty minutes. Baste every ten minutes with

Six tablespoons of vinegar,
Three-quarters tablespoon of boiling water.

Use the liquid in the pan, after baking the ham for making gravy, by browning three tablespoons of flour, then adding the liquid left in the pan and sufficient boiling water to make one and one-quarter cups of gravy. Season.

HAM LOAF

Chop the left-over ham very fine. Measure and add to one and one-half cups

One and one-half cups of cold cooked oatmeal,
Two onions, grated,
One teaspoon of paprika,
One-half cup of bread crumbs,
One cup of cream sauce,
One tablespoon of Worcestershire sauce.

Mix and then pour into well-greased loaf-shaped pan and then place this pan in a larger one containing warm water. Bake for forty minutes in a moderate oven. Serve with hot tomato sauce.

ENGLISH HAM PIE

Cut the remainder of the fresh baked ham into neat pieces, laying aside all the small bits. Pare and cut in dice sufficient potatoes to measure one quart. Chop fine sufficient onions to measure one cupful. Place the potatoes and onions in a saucepan and add sufficient boiling water to cover. Cook until tender and then drain. Now prepare a pastry as follows: Place

Two cups of flour,
One teaspoon of salt,
Two teaspoons of baking powder.

in a bowl. Sift and then rub in six tablespoons of shortening. Mix with one-half cup of ice-cold water. Roll out and then line a shallow pan with pastry. Place a layer of potatoes and onions and then a layer of the meat. Season well and cover the meat with a second layer of the potatoes. Season and then add two cups of highly seasoned gravy. Place top crust in position and fasten the edges tightly by pinching together firmly. Brush the pastry with cold water and then bake one hour in a slow oven.

CHEESE LOAF

Three cups of fine bread crumbs,
One and one-half cups of cottage cheese,
One and one-half cups of very thick cream sauce,
One large onion, minced fine,
One and one-half teaspoons of salt,
One teaspoon of paprika,
One teaspoon of Worcestershire sauce.

Mix thoroughly and then mould into shape. Pack into well-greased pan and set this pan in a large bake pan, with hot water to one-quarter of the depth of the bake pan. Bake in a moderate oven for fifty minutes.

BARBECUE OF BOILED HAM

Cut cold boiled ham into very thin slices and then place in a chafing dish and add

One-half glass of currant jelly,
Three tablespoons of vinegar,
Four tablespoons of water,
One-half teaspoon of Worcestershire sauce,
One-quarter teaspoon of paprika.

Heat until very hot, and then serve on toast.

HEAD CHEESE

Have the butcher clean and crack a young pig's head. Wash well and put on to cook in a pot large enough to have the water completely cover the head. Cook until the meat leaves the bones, skimming carefully. When cooked lift pot from the fire and take the meat from the pot. Chop fine, seasoning with salt and pepper and one tablespoon of poultry seasoning; mix thoroughly;

put a clean cloth in the colander and put in the cheese; cover with another cloth; place a plate on top and weight down with a flat-iron.

ITALIAN CANAPE

Mince fine

One green pepper,
One medium sized onion,
One leek,
Four branches of parsley,
One tomato.

Now place four tablespoons of shortening in a saucepan and add the vegetables. Cook slowly until tender and then add

Five tablespoons of grated cheese,
One teaspoon of salt,
One teaspoon of paprika.

Mix thoroughly and then spread on thin slices of toast. Garnish with sliced stuffed olives and dust with paprika.

CHEESE SAUCE

One cup of water,
One cup of milk,
Five level tablespoons of flour.

Dissolve the flour in milk and water; bring to a boil; cook slowly for ten minutes; now add

One teaspoon of salt,
One teaspoon of pepper,
One well-beaten egg,
One-half cup grated cheese.

WELSH RAREBIT

Cut one-half pound cheese very fine and then place in a saucepan and add

One-half teaspoon of mustard,
One teaspoon of grated onion,
Two well-beaten eggs,
One tablespoon of Worcestershire sauce.

Stir until well creamed and free from lumps and then pour over slices of toast. Sprinkle lightly with paprika and serve.

CHELSEA RABBIT

Cut one pound of cheese into small bits and then place two tablespoons of butter in a chafing dish and add

One onion, cut fine,
One cup of thick tomato pulp, pressed through a fine sieve,
One tablespoon of Worcestershire sauce,
One and one-half teaspoons of salt,
One and one-half teaspoons of paprika.

Cook until the onion is soft and then add cheese and stir until the cheese is melted and the mixture well blended. This will serve from six to eight persons.

CHEESE CANAPE

Place in a bowl

Three tablespoons of grated cheese,
One tablespoon of minced parsley,
One-quarter teaspoon of salt,
One-half teaspoon of paprika,
One tablespoon of butter.

Mix to a paste and then spread on a thin triangle of bread. Dust lightly with paprika.

TOMATO CANAPE

Cut the tomatoes into very thin slices and then place on a plate and season with salt and pepper. Now place on a plate

One tablespoon of butter,
One-half teaspoon of mustard,
One-quarter teaspoon of paprika,
One tablespoon of parsley.

Work to a nice smooth paste and then spread lightly over the tomatoes. Place on a small round cracker and garnish with a slice of hard-boiled egg.

LA BRETE CANAPE

Pick the fish from the backbone of a cooked mackerel, adding any left-over portions. There need be only about two tablespoons. Rub the fish through a sieve and add

One small onion, grated,
One-half teaspoon of mustard,
One-half teaspoon of paprika,
One and one-half tablespoons of butter.

Work to a paste and then spread on thin toasted strips of bread.

BOHEMIAN RELISH

Place on a bread and butter plate

Two slices of salomi sausage,
One radish,
One tablespoon of prepared scallion,
One thin slice of tomato.

To prepare the scallions chop fine and add

Six tablespoons of mayonnaise dressing,
One tablespoon of vinegar.

Mix thoroughly and then serve.

ITALIAN CANAPE

Two branches of parsley,
One small onion,
One-half green pepper.

Mince fine and then cook until soft, taking care not to brown, in two tablespoons of salad oil. Now toast thin slices of cornbread slightly and spread with this mixture. Sprinkle with grated cheese and paprika.

CANAPE A LA MODE

Flake into bits two tablespoons of the mackerel left from breakfast, and then place on a dish and add

Three tablespoons of mayonnaise dressing,
One teaspoon of paprika,
One tablespoon of finely chopped parsley.

Mix to a smooth paste and then spread on triangles of toasted bread. Garnish with parsley.

FRIED PIGS FEET

Have the butcher crack the feet; wash and put into a pot of boiling water to cook. Cook gently until they separate easily from the joints; lift from the water, and set to cool. When cold divide in portions, dip in egg and cracker-dust and fry in boiling hot lard. Serve with coleslaw or chow-chow.

MINCEMEAT

During the Xmas holidays open house was kept by the barons and knights of the early days. Great festivities and merrymaking was the order of the time. The great fête took place on Xmas day. On that day the mistresses of the households vied with each other in a friendly rivalry with their dishes of mutton pie.

The mutton pie, as it was known in 1596, is the mince pie of to-day. It was also known by the name of Xmas pie or shredds. In Herrick's time it was considered vitally important to put an armed guard to watch the Xmas pies, lest some sweet-toothed rascal purloin them and then there would be no pies to grace the feast. As ever in warring lands, food commodities were scarce and expensive and accordingly considered a great luxury.

MINCEMEAT

Mincemeat may now be prepared for the holidays; and if kept in a cool place it will have sufficient time to blend and ripen. Here are some inexpensive recipes:

One-half cup of suet,
One-half cup of grated carrot,
Six cups of apples, chopped fine,

Two cups of raisins, chopped,
One-half cup of cooked meat, chopped fine,
One-half cup of citron, chopped fine,
One-half cup of orange peel, chopped fine,
Two tablespoons of cinnamon,
One-half tablespoon of nutmeg,
One-half tablespoon of cloves,
One and one-half cups of molasses,
One cup of boiled cider.

Mix in the order given. Pack into a bowl or crock. Cover closely and then set in a cool place to ripen. Cold left-over meat may be used.

NEW ENGLAND MINCEMEAT

Place one-half pound of hamburg steak in a saucepan and add one cup of cider. Cook for fifteen minutes; then remove from the saucepan and place in a large bowl and add

Six ounces shredded suet,
One-half pound currants,
One-half pound of raisins,
Two pounds of minced apples,
Four ounces of minced citron,
Four ounces of minced orange peel,
Four ounces of minced lemon peel,
Two tablespoons of cinnamon,
One tablespoon of allspice,
Three-fourths of tablespoon of cloves,
Two and one-half cups of syrup,
One cup of boiled cider.

Mix in the order given, then pack in glass or crock. Cover closely and then set in a cool place to ripen.

ORANGE MINCEMEAT

Squeeze the juice of three oranges. Place the peel in a saucepan of cold water. Cook until tender. Drain and then pour through the food chopper. Place in a bowl and add

Six cups of apples, chopped moderately fine,
One cup of suet, chopped fine,
One cup of raisins, chopped fine,
One cup of evaporated peaches, chopped fine,
One cup of evaporated apricots, chopped fine,
One-half cup of citron, chopped fine,
One cup of grated carrot,
Two tablespoons of cinnamon,
One-half tablespoon of allspice,
One-half tablespoon of mace,
One-half tablespoon of ginger,
One-half tablespoon of cloves,
Two cups of molasses,
One cup of boiled cider.

Mix in the order given and then pack in a large bowl or crock or stone pot. Cover closely and then put in a cool place for ten days to ripen.

GREEN TOMATO AND APPLE MINCE

Place one quart of green tomatoes chopped fine in a colander. Cover with two tablespoons of salt. Let drain for two hours. Place in a saucepan and add

One cup of syrup,
One cup of cider.

Cook gently for one-half hour; now pour into a bowl and add

Three-fourths of a cup of shredded suet,
Five cups of apples, chopped,
One carrot, grated fine,
Two cups of raisins, chopped fine,
Two cups of dates, chopped fine,

One-half cup of figs, chopped fine,
One-half cup of peanuts, chopped fine,
One and one-half tablespoons of cinnamon,
One-half tablespoon of cloves,
One-half tablespoon of nutmeg,
One-half tablespoon of ginger,
One and one-half cups of molasses,
One cup of boiled cider.

Mix in the order given; then store as directed in the preceding recipes. Do not peel the apples. When putting the suet, raisins and dried fruit through the food chopper, add a dried crust of bread to prevent clogging.

EGGS

The similarity in the proportion of the shell, yolk and white of eggs in the chicken eggs is that the shell averages about one-tenth, the yolk about three-fourths and the white about four-tenths. The shell alone is counted as waste. The white contains about six-eighths water, the solids of the white are virtually all nitrogenous matter or protein. The yolk contains about one-half water and one-third fat, and the balance is of nitrogenous matter or protein.

Newly laid or fresh eggs have a semi-transparent uniform, pale pinkish tint; the shell contains a very small air chamber, which separates the skin and shell of the egg and is filled with air. This chamber increases with the age of the egg.

Eggs when cooked at a low temperature are delicate and easy to digest, and they can be used for invalids, and persons with a delicate digestion.

HOW TO COOK EGGS

Eggs boiled are eggs spoiled; the physicians tell us that hard-boiled eggs require three and a half hours to digest. Keep this in mind when cooking eggs. Water boils at a temperature of 212 degrees Fahrenheit. Eggs should be cooked at a temperature between 165 and 185 degrees Fahrenheit.

Place water in a saucepan and bring to a boil; boil for three minutes and add the eggs. Place on the back of the stove and let the eggs stand for eight minutes for a very soft boil and twenty-five minutes for hard boiled. The water should be kept hot—that is, just below the boiling point.

FRIED EGGS

Place the fat in the pan and heat until very hot and then place where the pan will maintain this heat without getting any hotter; if you use the gas turn down the burner. Add the eggs. Let them cook very slowly until set and then turn if desired. Eggs cooked in this way will not absorb the fat and will be tender and delicate, and not have a crust of crisped egg around the edge.

EGGS CARTHEOTH

Tomatoes, peppers and pimentoes are generally used for this dish. Prepare the tomatoes or peppers by cutting a slice from the top and then hollowing out the centers. Break in an egg and then season with salt and pepper and a little finely minced parsley. Cover with two tablespoons of cream sauce. Place in the oven and bake for ten minutes. Finely minced ham or bacon may be sprinkled over the egg before adding the cream sauce.

Cold cooked or left-over vegetables, such as corn, peas, asparagus, onions or cauliflower, may be used also. Cold boiled potatoes, beets, turnips, etc., may be made to do duty in place of tomatoes, peppers or pimentos for the sake of variety. Serve with a thick, highly seasoned sauce.

POACHED EGGS

To prepare poached eggs place water in a saucepan and add one tablespoon of vinegar to each pint of water. Bring to a boil and then open the egg on a saucer and slide into the boiling water, let simmer slowly until it forms and then lift with a skimmer on to a napkin to drain. Then roll gently on a slice of buttered toast.

If you have any old-fashioned muffin rings place them flat in the bottom of the saucepan and then pour the eggs in and poach. Or you may use any of the poachers, that are sold in any of the house-furnishing stores.

OMELET

Plain and fluffy omelets are cooked in the same manner as the fried eggs.

PLAIN OMELET

Place three tablespoons of shortening in a frying pan and then, while heating, place the three eggs in a bowl and add

One tablespoon of milk,
One tablespoon of water.

Beat with a fork to thoroughly mix and then, when the pan is smoking hot, turn in the mixture. Then place where the omelet will cook very slowly. Season and then turn and fold and roll, turning on a hot platter.

SPANISH OMELET

Use the fluffy omelet recipe and then chop fine two medium-sized tomatoes, drain free from the moisture and add one medium-sized onion and four large olives, chopped fine. Place in a small pan with one tablespoon of butter to heat. When hot spread over the omelet and then fold and roll or place in a hot oven and bake.

FLUFFY OMELET

Separate the yolks and whites of three eggs. Place the yolks in a bowl and add three tablespoons of milk. Beat to thoroughly mix and then beat the whites until very stiff. Cut and fold the yolks into the prepared whites and then turn into a pan and cook slowly. Fold and roll and turn on a hot platter.

Fried eggs and omelets may be garnished with ham, bacon, parsley, finely chopped; pimentos and green peppers.

To make variously flavored omelets, prepare the omelet as for plain omelet and then just before the turning and rolling add the desired flavoring. Then roll and fold the omelet and turn out on a hot dish. Have the filling heated before spreading on the omelet. Left-over vegetables and bits of meat may be used in this manner for attractive dishes.

TIGER-EYE SANDWICHES

Use strictly fresh eggs for this. Separate the white and the yolk and keep the yolk in the shell until ready for use. Add a pinch of salt to the white and beat until very stiff. Pile in a pyramid on a square slice of toast. Make a well in the centre of the white of egg and then drop in the yolk. Dust over lightly with paprika and then bake for seven minutes in a hot oven.

MEASUREMENTS

Many women are familiar with the importance of accurate measurements in preparing foods. Others frequently complain of the troubles they have with recipes, but what they actually need to know is that we no longer live in the days of twenty-five cents a dozen for fresh eggs and that the day of thirty cents per pound for creamery butter of excellent quality is past.

Gone are the days of plenty when the extravagant cook was the best cook. Banish all recipes that call for cups of butter.

From motives of real practical economy, we now use level measurements; that means that you first sift your flour into a bowl and then fill the measure, using a spoon to fill with and then level the top of the measure with a knife. Level measurement means all that lies below the edge of the cup or spoon.

The experienced cook with an eye for measurements can gauge the amounts, very frequently, to a nicety. While she may sometimes have a failure, she will never attribute it to her measure or the method of compounding the ingredients; oftentimes she will blame the flour, the baking powder or even the oven.

One woman wrote me that she wished to know what the trouble was with her cakes. I asked her to give the recipe and she answered that she generally used a bowl for measuring and that then she used sugar, eggs, butter, flour and enough milk or water to make a batter—there was no real definite amounts. When I replied I told her that it was the measurements and methods that she used that frequently caused a failure. But she was sure that was not the case, for her cake was usually good, and it was only once in a while that she had a failure. So I had quite a time convincing her that accurate measurements will always give the same results and assured success and that she could bake the same cake 365 days in the year and not once have a failure.

To-day this woman would not return to the old way of doing her cooking, and recently I had a little note from her telling me to let the other middle-aged and young housewives, too, know how necessary it is to be accurate.

You know it only takes a few minutes longer to measure accurately, and then you are able to make that delicious cake without a failure. No failures, no waste. Truly, the words of "trusting to luck" should be taboo in the efficient woman's kitchen.

The temptation to add just a little more sugar, flour or shortening to a recipe with the idea of improving it must be eliminated if you wish to cook successfully. When using vegetable oil in place of butter in making cakes cut down the quantity of fat fully one-third. Many cake recipes contain too much fat.

When the amounts are less than one cup, frequently it is easier to measure with a spoon. Remember all measures are level:

Sixteen tablespoons	1 cup
Eight tablespoons	½ cup
Four tablespoons	¼ cup
Five tablespoons plus one teaspoon	⅓ cup

Sift the flour once before measuring. Standard measuring cups holding one-half pint are divided on one side into quarters and on the other side into thirds, and they are usually found in all housefurnishing stores, and there is a choice of aluminum, glass or tin.

Sets of measuring spoons will save time and trouble. The spoons graduate from one-quarter of a teaspoon to one tablespoon, thus making accurate measurements for seasoning and flavoring.

A spatula will repay its cost many times over the first month it is used. It is possible with this knife to remove every particle of food from a mixing bowl.

How can you keep a house without a pair of reliable scales? Do you know how much the chicken weighed that you bought on Saturday, and do you know how much waste there was; or the weight of the bone in the meat that you purchased on Wednesday? Do you ever weigh your purchases? Think this over and then buy a good pair of scales and keep them in a convenient place.

List of equivalent measures:—

1 salt spoon	¼ teaspoon
3 teaspoons	1 tablespoon
3 tablespoons	1 cooking spoon
4 tablespoons	¼ cup
8 tablespoons	½ cup
12 tablespoons	¾ cup
16 tablespoons	1 cup
2 cups	1 pint
2 pints	1 quart
4 quarts	1 gallon

DRY MEASURE

8 quarts	1 peck
2 quarts	¼ peck
4 quarts	½ peck
2 cups granulated sugar	1 pound
2¾ cups brown sugar	1 pound
3½ cups ground coffee	1 pound
3 cups of cornstarch	1 pound

2 cups of butter	1 pound
2 cups of lard	1 pound
3 cups granulated cornmeal	1 pound
3¾ cups of rye flour	1 pound
3¾ cups of graham flour	1 pound
3¾ cups of unsifted wheat flour	1 pound
4 cups of sifted flour	1 pound
3½ cups whole wheat flour	1 pound
9 cups of bran flour	1 pound
2 cups of rice flour	1 pound

ITALIAN DRESSING

One-half cup of salad oil,
Four tablespoons of vinegar,
One teaspoon of salt,
One teaspoon of paprika,
Three tablespoons of grated cheese.

Place in a fruit jar and then shake to blend.

SOUR CREAM CUCUMBER DRESSING

Pare and grate one medium-sized cucumber and then sprinkle with one teaspoon of salt. Let stand for one hour and then drain, and place one cup of sour cream in a bowl. Beat until stiff and add the prepared cucumber and

One teaspoon of mustard,
One teaspoon of pepper,
Two tablespoons of finely chopped onion,
Two tablespoons of finely chopped parsley,
Juice of one-half lemon.

Mix well before serving.

CREAM CABBAGE

Cut the cabbage fine and then place in cold salted water to crisp. Drain well and then add

One green or red pepper, chopped fine to each quart of cabbage,
One tablespoon of mustard seed

and then prepare a dressing as follows:

Place in a soup plate the yolk of one egg, and then add

One teaspoon of vinegar,
One teaspoon of mustard,
One teaspoon of sugar,
One teaspoon of paprika.

Work with a fork to a smooth thick paste, and then add slowly one-half cup of salad oil. When very thick reduce to the desired consistency with four tablespoons of evaporated milk and six to eight tablespoons of vinegar. Beat with a Dover egg-beater and then pour over the cabbage.

SALADS

Wash and drain the lettuce and then shred fine, using a pair of sharp scissors. Place in a bowl and then chop fine one bunch of scallions and a stalk of celery and add to the lettuce. Cover with mayonnaise dressing and serve for luncheon with a plate of cream soup. Toast and a light dessert will complete this meal.

ENGLISH WATER-CRESS SALAD

Cut five strips of bacon in dice and then brown nicely in a frying pan. Lift cooked bacon, drain off the fat, leaving only about five tablespoons in the pan. Now place in a cup

One-half teaspoon of mustard,
One-half teaspoon of sugar,
One teaspoon of salt,

One-half teaspoon of paprika,
Four tablespoons of vinegar.

Dissolve and pour into the hot fat, bring to a boil and then add the cooked bacon. Now place the prepared water-cress in a bowl and pour over it the bacon with the prepared dressing. Toss gently to mix and then garnish with hard-boiled eggs (sliced).

Corn salad, cabbage, lettuce, romaine and escarolle salads may be used in place of the water-cress for variety.

Radishes should be well washed and then allowed to crisp in cold water. Split from the tip to the stem end in quarters. Large radishes may be peeled and cooked until tender in boiling water and then drained and served with a cream, Hollandaise or plain butter sauce for variety.

OLD ENGLISH MUSTARD DRESSING

One tablespoon of evaporated milk,
One teaspoon of mustard.

Place in a soup plate and blend together, then add one tablespoon of oil. Then drop the vinegar, then the oil again until you have used

Eight tablespoons of salad oil,
One tablespoon of vinegar.

Serve on lettuce, cucumbers, meat or fish.

RICH BOILED SALAD DRESSING

One-half cup of water,
Three-quarters cup of vinegar,
Five tablespoons of cornstarch.

Dissolve the starch in water and bring to a boil. Cook for three minutes and then add

One well-beaten egg,
One-half cup of thick cream,
One tablespoon of sugar,
One teaspoon of salt,
One teaspoon of paprika.

Mix the sugar and seasoning with the cream and add the egg; then add to the boiling mixture and remove from the fire at once. Beat in slowly six tablespoons of salad oil. This will keep in a cool place for six weeks.

ASPARAGUS VINAIGRETTE

Wash and scrape the asparagus and allow four stalks for each service. Trim to remove the pithy end of the stalk and then cook in boiling water until tender. Lift and drain well, then place in a dish and cover with the following sauce:

Four tablespoons of salad oil,
Two tablespoons of vinegar,
One-half tablespoon of grated onion,
One-half tablespoon of finely chopped green pepper,
One teaspoon of salt,
One teaspoon of paprika,
One-quarter teaspoon of mustard.

Beat to mix and then set on ice to chill. Serve ice cold on crisp lettuce leaves.

www.ingramcontent.com/pod-product-compliance
Lightning Source LLC
Chambersburg PA
CBHW081623100526
44590CB00021B/3569